Portugal

BY PETER WHELPTON

Published by COLLINS London and Glasgow
   and by RAND McNALLY Chicago, New York, San Francisco
Library of Congress Catalog Card Number: 67:10638

Drawings by BARBARA CROCKER
Maps by BROAD OAK STUDIOS
Design and Layout by RONALD MONGREDIEN
Photographs by courtesy of BARNABY'S PICTURE LIBRARY (*page 63*);
   PORTUGUESE STATE OFFICE (*page 80*); COMISSARIADO DO TURISMO
   LISBON (*frontispiece; pages 17, 24, 38, 53, 56, 69, 78*)

CONTENTS

See overleaf for list of maps

MAPS

*Map references for each town will be found
in the Index*

ABBREVIATIONS

c.c.	cubic centimetre(s)	lb	pound(s)
esc	escudo(s)	Max	maximum
grm	gram(s)	Min	minimum
in	inch(es)	oz	ounce(s)
kilo	kilogram	pop.	population
kilos	kilograms	sq.	square
km	kilometre(s)	temp	temperature

A.A.	Automobile Association
A.A.A.	American Automobile Association
R.A.C.	Royal Automobile Club

INTRODUCTION

Portugal has an enormous amount to offer the visitor. The climate is such that fine weather, blue skies and sunshine can be guaranteed, yet the weather, tempered by breezes from the Atlantic, is seldom so hot as to be unpleasant. The hotel situation has improved tremendously over the past few years, and there is a wide variety of accommodation to suit all tastes and pockets. Life is cheap, too, especially the little luxuries that are so much part of a good holiday. A bottle of wine, a basket of strawberries, a taxi when you are tired—these are some of the luxuries that in Portugal become everyday affairs.

Above all, it is the people that make a country. In Portugal you will find a people who is friendly, courteous and gentle. Ask a Portuguese the way, and he will invariably take you to your destination. Pass a farmer in his fields, and more often than not he will offer you a bunch of grapes or a few figs. Sit next to a family in a train, and you will be sharing their bread, wine and cheese before you know what is happening.

Portugal is a country of contrasts. The Douro and the Minho regions of the north might be in a different country to the Algarve. Half-an-hour's drive from the sophistication of Estoril you can be in a country village where the main means of transportation is the donkey. Inland, there is a wealth of excitement and discovery for the student of art and architecture; while for the sun-lover there are miles of unspoilt beaches. If you can go in the spring or autumn, rather than in the high season, all the better. Prices will be lower, hotels less crowded, and in spring, in particular, you will have the benefit of the mimosa and the almond blossom.

Wherever you go, the Portuguese will make you welcome. They are natural hosts, proud of their country and anxious to show it to the best advantage, especially to their oldest allies.

THE PEOPLE, MANNERS AND CUSTOMS

The Portuguese are a courteous, gentle race, fond of formality and with an over-riding air of melancholy typified in the *fado* [fah´doo]. They will show the utmost good manners and kindness to a complete stranger, but, given offence by a good friend, can be touchy in the extreme. They are home-loving, but rarely ask anyone but close relatives to their houses. The men carry out much of their social and business life in the cafés. The women stay at home, looking after their large families, and in their spare moments gossiping on the balcony or at the doorway. In middle-class

Portuguese fisherwomen

families there will be two or three maid servants, and the lady of the house will meet her friend at a tea-shop. Even so, in spite of the increasing number of women graduates, Portugal is still to a great extent a masculine society. In the north and in the Algarve it is quite common to see a man riding on his donkey while his wife trudges along behind.

The Portuguese are great lovers of children. Even in the poorest districts the little girls will be lovingly, dressed for church on Sundays in layer upon layer of starched frilly petticoats under an immaculate white dress. The little boys wear white shirts and shorts, topped with a white jockey-style cap. Occasionally you will be asked for money by children in the poorer districts. It is wiser and kinder not to succumb. First, you will have all the children in the neighbourhood around you, and, secondly, the proud Portuguese don't approve of their children accepting money.

When dealing with Portuguese friends, a considerable degree of formality is usual. Even when addressing servants, it is customary to ask a favour, rather than demand a service. In speaking, it is usual to call men by their surnames, preceded by *O Senhor* [oo se-nyohr']. In the case of ladies, you use the surname preceded by *Senhora dona* [se-nyoh'rå doh'nå]. It is a matter of courtesy in Portugal to use degrees and titles when addressing people in conversation. Anyone who has obtained a degree in any subject is addressed as *Senhor doutor* [se-nyohr' doh-tohr'], followed by christian name and surname. The same applies to the title of engineer, *Senhor engenheiro* [se-nyohr' en-zhe-nyay'ee-roo], and titles such as *director* [dee-re-tohr'], *administrador* [ad-mee-nish-trå-dohr'], and *chefe* [shef]. In writing, you address men as *Exmo.Senhor,* or, in the case of business letters, *Illmo. Senhor.*

The Portuguese are an intensely religious and modest race. Great care should be taken not to offend local susceptibilities in the question of dress. Women should wear shorts and slacks only in the streets of resorts and both sexes should have long sleeves when entering churches. Ladies should cover their heads with a scarf or handkerchief.

Finally, one little matter of manners peculiar to Portugal: it is extremely rude to stretch.

A BRIEF HISTORY

The history of Portugal from the arrival of the first Iberians in the Penin-sula some 2,000 years before Christ to the establishment of Doctor Salazar as premier in 1932 is as complex as that of any European state, and as you travel round Portugal today you will see traces of Roman and Greek occupation, of the Mozarabic civilisation centred on Coimbra and, particularly in the Algarve, the racial influence of slaves brought back from Africa during Portugal's great period of expansion. Many names are part Iberian, part Arabic and in the north place names such as Taipas recall the Visigothic occupation.

Portugal has existed as an independent state since the 12th century and was, indeed, the first of the European states to become consolidated into one unit. Until that date it shared a more or less common history with the rest of the Iberian Peninsula and after the arrival of the Iberians was colonised by the Phoenicians, the Greeks and the Romans (218 B.C.). Even at that time a tribe dwelling in what was to become the province of Minho offered extremely violent resistance to the Romans and fought as far away as Andalusia in south-eastern Spain. The leader of this tribe, the Lusitanians, was called Viriatus and his name is still spoken of with affection in Portugal. Under M. Vipsianus Agrippa the whole Peninsula was divided into three provinces (27 B.C.) and the westernmost one, which included most of modern Portugal but extended into Spain, was named Lusitania. During the Roman occupation the country enjoyed compara-tive peace and Braga and Évora—where the ruins of the Temple to Diana are still to be seen—as well as many other cities were built. A settlement on the Douro known as Portus Cale (Oporto) gave its name to the country, although it originally applied to the area between the Douro and the Galician border formed by the river Minho. After the Germanic invasion (409-418), the Suebi maintained an independent kingdom in the north-west, but this was incorporated into Visigothic Spain in 585 A.D. From this time until the Moorish invasion in 711 relatively little is known of the history of the Peninsula although many of the Goths were converted to Christianity and the inhabitants were not to suffer the persecution later inflicted on the Jews in the 15th and 16th centuries.

Although the Moors were to exercise a profound cultural influence on the southern part of the Peninsula they never successfully colonised the north and by the 10th century Portugal north of the Douro was a province ruled over by the house of Léon in Spain. By 1064 Ferdinand I of Castile and Léon had driven the Moors back to the Mondego, capturing Coimbra and appointing a separate governor. From 1109 Portugal was fought over by the house of Léon and the descendants of Alphonso VI's (1065-1109) illegitimate daughter and her husband, Henry, who had been granted the territory in 1095. In 1143 Alphonso Henriques, a cousin of the king of Léon, obtained the independence of the territory and during the next hundred years he and his successors were largely occupied in completing the conquest of the rest of Portugal from the Moors and gained control of the provinces of Alentejo and Algarve. During the reigns of Alphonso III of Portugal (1248-1279) and Diniz (1279-1325) important institutional advances took place and Portugal proper commenced its development as an independent state. It came into closer contact with western Europe and acquired a university (at Coimbra), the elements of a national literature and a navy. Nonetheless there were still disputes with Castile, largely occasioned by Diniz's son Alphonso IV (1325-57) before and after his accession despite the efforts of his mother, Isabella. This remarkable woman later canonised as St. Elizabeth of Portugal and popularly known as a *Rainha-Santa* (Queen Saint), was buried at Coimbra where her silver and crystal tomb is preserved in the new church of the Monastery of Santa Clara.

The reigns of Pedro I (1357-67), popularly known as 'the Just' for his interest in justice and his somewhat arbitrary administration of it (see also ALCOBAÇA), his son Ferdinand I and his illegitimate son, John I

Castle on the Rio Tejo

of Aviz, were to see the establishment of firm links with England by marriage (see page 52) and with Flanders by trade and the start of the great age of Portuguese expansion with the conquest of Ceuta in Morocco (1415).

Events at home over the next 160 years were relatively uncomplicated and the house of Aviz continued to have its representatives on the throne despite the usual intrigues characteristic of this period of European history. Attempts were made to unite the crowns of Castile and Portugal, each country in turn hoping to achieve dominance over the other, and Manoel I (1495-1521) who inherited a firmly established monarchy and an expanding overseas empire from John II, John I's great-grandson, even produced a son from his marriage with Maria, eldest daughter of Ferdinand and Isabella of Castile. This son was recognised as legitimate heir to the thrones of Portugal, Castile and Aragón but he died in infancy and, since his mother had died giving birth to him, nothing came of the proposed union. This unusual period of stability and security came to an end in the reign of Sebastião (1557-78) who had been obsessed with the idea of a crusade against the Moors from his earliest years. The expedition ended in disaster, the king and 8,000 men were killed and a further 15,000 were captured. In the ensuing chaos, hardly tempered by the short reign of the aged and celibate Cardinal Henriques, Sebastião's great-uncle, Philip II, prepared for the invasion of Portugal. Henriques died in 1580 and in 1581 an army under the celebrated duke of Alba entered Portugal, Philip proclaimed himself Philip I of Portugal, all other claims to the throne were ignored and Britain and Holland were able to seize large parts of Portugal's empire.

Portugal's history, like that of every country, was partly determined by its geographical position. Bound on two sides by an almost consistently hostile Spain, Portugal naturally turned to the sea once she had achieved a national identity. It was the sea that had brought hints of strange far-away countries to her shores and it was by sea that this tiny nation whose population was somewhat less than half a million in the 15th century acquired a great empire. Not only did Portugal become extremely wealthy as she began to exploit her overseas territories but this period of discovery was instrumental in forming the national architecture of Portugal, which is characterised by marine decoration. Good examples of this style and approach are to be found at Belém, the Monastery of Batalha and in the cloisters of the Monastery of Santa Cruz at Coimbra.

Prince Henry the Navigator (1394-1460), who played a decisive role in the capture of Ceuta, was the guiding mind behind the Portuguese expansion and from his base at Sagres near Cape St. Vincent in the Algarve equipped a series of expeditions which during his lifetime re-discovered the Azores and started colonisation there and explored the African coast and some of the interior as far as Sierra Leone. Although he forbade the capture and sale of slaves, the trade was carried on after his death and it is from this time that can be dated the introduction of

Cape St. Vincent

African blood into the southern part of Portugal. Henry's great achievement was to codify the information brought back by his sailors into charts and tables and to provide future explorers with navigational instruments which were to assist Bartolemeu Diaz de Novaes to round the Cape of Good Hope in 1488, Vasco da Gama to reach India in 1498 and Pedro Alvares Cabral to claim Brazil for Portugal in 1500 at a time when English explorers had hardly put to sea. The greatest of all explorers, a man who ranks with Columbus, Marco Polo and Henry himself, was also a Portuguese—Magellan—who was the first man to sail round the world (1519-21), dying during the voyage. Although this voyage was carried out under the auspices of Spain, as was Columbus's discovery of America, an event which by no means overshadows Magellan's achievement, both men owed much to Henry's research.

For nearly a century Portugal controlled the trade to the Orient with a series of strongpoints from the Persian Gulf to Malacca on the Malay Peninsula. Settlements were founded which extended from Bengal to China and the trade of the principal spice islands was in Portuguese hands. Although the Portuguese suffered several reverses, their control of the oriental trade remained substantial until the 17th century when the Dutch, at war with the crowns of Spain and Portugal and deprived of their traditional trade with Lisboa, demolished the Portuguese monopoly.

Portugal was administered by the Spanish crown until 1640 when with the assistance of a revolt in Catalonia, the Franco/Spanish war and Richelieu's agents in Lisboa, the Spanish garrisons were driven out and the duke of Braganza (Bragança) was crowned John IV. The event is commemorated by an obelisk in the Praça dos Restauradores in Lisboa. It was not, however, until 1668 that Spain finally recognised Portuguese independence and by this time a further alliance had been concluded with England on the marriage of Charles II and Catherine of Braganza, John's daughter. Her dowry included both Tangiers and Bengal. Portuguese prosperity now began to increase as gold and precious stones poured in from Brazil and many royal palaces, academies and libraries were built. The great Palace of Queluz, the library at Coimbra and the Palace of Freixo in Porto are examples of this architectural flowering encouraged by greater national wealth.

Throughout the 18th century the *cortes*—a vaguely democratic body similar to the French estates, which was summoned at the king's pleasure —was not called upon and after a brief attempt at government through a council of ministers under John V (1706-50) Portugal sank into stagnation. However, on the accession of Joseph (1750-77), Sebastião José de Carvalho e Mello, later the Marquis of Pombal, was appointed chief minister and governed until Joseph's death. Although he can only charitably be called an 'enlightened' despot he carried through reforms in every branch of commerce, founded new industries and was responsible for the rebuilding of Lisboa after the terrible earthquake of 1755. The most impressive feature of the new city was the Praça do Comércio, known to the English as Black Horse Square after the equestrian statue of Joseph there, which is a fitting monument to the achievements and vision of a man who was active on every administrative front from the army to the development of Brazil.

Portugal remained virtually unmolested during the Napoleonic Wars until 1807, despite being under continual pressure to break off her alliance with England. Late in 1807 as a result of Napoleon's wish to blockade all continental ports to English ships, the French and the Spanish invaded Portugal, and the royal family together with John, the prince regent, was evacuated to Brazil by the British, Portugal suffered two further invasions and the French were finally driven out by Wellington in 1811 (see page 60). The Napoleonic campaigns had caused great devastation in Portugal and this, together with the absence of the royal family and the general feeling of liberalism throughout Europe released by the French Revolution and the collapse of the *ancien régime,* produced an atmosphere of restlessness. The Portuguese were never slow to show dissatisfaction with the status quo. Despite the efforts of the British in Portugal under William Beresford, John, now John VI, returned only in 1821 to find himself bound to a new 'democratic' constitution. His eldest son, Pedro, he left to govern Brazil and in due course Pedro appointed himself emperor of Brazil. It proved impossible to find a ruler who would prove acceptable to all the political parties after John's death in 1826, and the country was torn by risings and wars between and in support of rival branches of the Braganza family, until the Duque de Saldanha took over the government in 1851. There followed nearly 40 years of peace, but by 1900 Portugal had been involved in disputes with Britain over her colonies which had resulted in governmental resignations and desperate efforts on the part of the ruling house to maintain control, and she was in considerable financial difficulties. The Republican party gained steadily in strength, and late in 1910 Manoel II fled to England, where he lived in Twickenham, and in the summer of 1911 a new constitution was passed after a general election.

Peace, however, was not to come until the election of General Carmona as president of the republic in 1928, for the republican party on achieving power immediately divided into the usual three factions, assassinations and revolts were not infrequent, the army began to play an important part in politics and little was achieved except for the founding of the universities of Lisboa and Porto. By 1928 over 40 cabinets had been formed and had resigned, but with the appointment of Doctor Salazar, professor of law at Coimbra university, as finance minister, Portugal entered on a period of security and increasing prosperity. Between 1928 and 1940 Salazar produced an unbroken series of budgetary surpluses and Portugal's currency is now one of the safest in the world. Although Portugal had supplied an expeditionary force during the first world war, Doctor Salazar, who assumed absolute power in 1932, practised a form of neutrality during World War II which was entirely compatible with the long-standing Anglo-Portuguese alliance.

That Doctor Salazar is a dictator is undeniable. But he has been a benevolent dictator. While freedom for the opposition and criticism of the régime in the press and by the public have been denied, the benefits that have accrued from his administration in a country with a long history of anarchy and instability are there for all to see. In the past 20 years the peasant's lot has been much improved. Illiteracy is fast declining and fine roads, hospitals, schools and parks have been built. Tourism, wine, cork, dried fruit, sardines and minerals are some of the industries that have expanded dramatically over the past two decades, enabling Portugal once again to take her rightful place amongst the nations of the world.

LITERATURE, ART AND ARCHITECTURE

The artistic, literary and architectural achievements of Portugal are largely unfamiliar to the English-speaking peoples owing to a dearth of translations and studies of the art of this nation. Throughout Portugal there are many outstanding buildings which compare favourably with other more celebrated examples of western architecture. Portuguese literature has produced some of the greatest works of our civilisation. It is true that the Portuguese genius has been criticised for its ready adaptation

Cork oaks

and assimilation of foreign influences, but this is characteristic of an
outward-looking nation and to be preferred to the parochialism of much
contemporary English literature, for example. Portuguese architects and
poets have shown that they possess a genuine native gift and character of
their own and, although it will be possible to mention only the most
prominent examples of their work in the following pages, it should
become clear that Portugal does not deserve to be ignored in any discus-
sion of architecture or literature.

Architecture

The architecture of Portugal is rich and varied, ranging from the remains
of the Temple to Diana in Évora to the magnificent bridge now being
built across the Tagus in Lisboa. There are few traces of the Greek,
Roman, Visigothic and Moorish occupations, but in the remarkably
rich town of Évora there are traces of Roman and Moorish walls. At
Braga, an important centre from the 2nd century B.C. to the 8th century
A.D., there are several remains which show a strong Germanic influence,
and the 7th-century church of São Pedro de Balsemão near Lamego is
probably the oldest in Portugal.

With the introduction of the Romanesque style to Portugal, reflecting
the establishment of the Church's power in public life, several impressive
buildings were designed, including the Old Cathedral at Coimbra with its
fine western portal and the Templar's Church at Tomar. At Braga and
Porto, too, fine Romanesque cathedrals were built but, as with so much
of Portuguese architecture, the one received extensive Manueline modi-
fications in the 16th century and the other was almost entirely renewed

in the 17th and 18th centuries. In Porto the charming little church of São
Martinho de Cedofeita is also worth a visit. It is, however, with the early
introduction of the Gothic style that Portuguese architecture enters its
period of greatness, and it is hard to believe that the term Gothic was
coined as a word of abuse in northern Italy during the Renaissance
when one visits the vast Cistercian monastery at Alcobaça which has,
exceptionally, remained unaltered, or the Cathedral at Évora.

The greatest Gothic building in Portugal is at Batalha. The Mosteiro
de Santa Maria de Vitória was founded by John I in thanksgiving for his
victory over the Castilians (1388) which secured Portuguese independence
(*batalha* = battle). The Monastery is a combination of mature Gothic and
Portuguese Gothic or Manueline architecture and took some 170 years
to complete. The Church, however, which was finished before 1433 is
pure Gothic and forms an exquisite contrast to the voluptuous style of
much of the rest of the building. The Manueline style, named after
Manoel I (1495-1521), is the most truly Portuguese of those to be found
in the great buildings of Portugal and is typified by an abundance of
decorative detail reflecting the maritime age to which it belongs. The
predominant features are ropes, shells, anchors, seaweeds, exotic plants
and many details borrowed from the sumptuous decorations on Indian
and Moorish buildings. The chief exponents of this style are Mateus
Fernandes who worked at Batalha and was probably responsible for the
magnificent Claustro Real; Boytaca who designed the lovely Convento
dos Jerónimos de Belém; and João de Castilho who not only completed

Lisboa: Tower of Belém

Batalha but also executed Boytaco's designs at Belém and built the Cloisters there which are, perhaps, his greatest achievement.

Throughout Portugal you will find other examples of Manueline architecture. Viana do Castelo is rich in buildings with Manueline balconies, windows and decorations. The Tower of Belém (Bethlehem), which was originally built to protect the mouth of the river Tagus but subsequently became a prison, is pure Manueline as is the Church of São João Baptista (1490) in Tomar with its fantastic and elegant portal. The Palace at Sintra was started in the 14th century but, although it has many Moorish and late-Gothic elements, it was completed in the Manueline style and many other buildings were modified or decorated in accordance with the current fashion. In Lisboa there is the Church of Nossa Senhora de Conceição Velha which, although largely destroyed in 1755, still retains its ornate Manueline façade. It was rebuilt in the current 18th-century style which forms an interesting contrast with the original façade. Indeed, one of the delights of Portuguese architecture is the wide variety of design that is found within the same building. Possibly the last manifestation of the Manueline style is the fantastic folly of Carlos's hunting lodge at Buçaco which was built in the 1880s.

During the 16th century, the Italian Renaissance was to exercise a strong influence on Portuguese architecture, both indirectly through assimilation and directly through artists from Lombardy who came to work in Portugal. Afonso Alvares designed the remarkable Cathedral of Portalegre which also contains 18th-century elements as does his Cathedral at Leiria. He was responsible for the Church of São Roque in Lisboa which was built for the Jesuits in 1566. The captivity of Portugal (1580-1640) was to stifle much of her creative power and the most influential architect of the time was Filippo Terzi, an Italian, who designed many fine late-Renaissance buildings. He had originally been summoned by Philip II to supervise the erection of fortifications, but his important work is to be seen at the Bishop's Palace in Coimbra which he rebuilt and the Church of São Vicente de Fora (1582-1627) in Lisboa with its lavishly decorated interior.

Elsewhere, Portuguese architects were coming under the influence of the French and were constructing lighter and simpler buildings such as the dainty Sacristy of the Mosteiro de Santa Cruz. During the latter half of the 17th century Portuguese architecture tends to be rather ponderous and monotonous and the only light notes come from gilt wood carvings such as you may find in the Church of São Francisco in Porto. The silver Altar do Sacramento in the Cathedral in Porto and the finely proportioned fountain in the late-Renaissance Claustro de João III of the Templar's Church in Tomar are two of the best examples of Portuguese achievements in the early 17th century.

However, by the middle of the 17th century the Renaissance, which had been distinguished by its reversion to classical forms and proportions, was losing its vigour, although its influence was to persist in

England till the 19th century. The new impulse came again from Italy, initially from Rome, and received the name Baroque.

Baroque architecture emphasised movement, variation, and elegant decoration, becoming the foremost style of the period, and in Portugal an important feature was the use of *azulejos*—glazed coloured tiles imported from Seville in the 15th century. Originally they were decorated in all colours, but by the 18th century their character had changed and the tiles were mostly blue and white, depicting the lives of saints and hunting and battle scenes. Nonetheless, the most striking building of this period was the vast and bleak Monastery of Mafra which was designed by Johann Friedrich Ludwig and his son, Johann Peter Ludwig, both of whom came from Regensberg. The Monastery was commissioned by John V in 1717 and was completed in 1735. It includes a church, a palace and the monastic buildings themselves, but it is merely spectacular rather than beautiful.

The Palace of Queluz (1758-92), on the other hand, is one of the most attractive buildings in Portugal and is set in an elegant park just outside Lisboa. Built of pink stone and bearing some resemblance to the Petit Trianon, it has been decorated with gaiety and colour by Reinaldo Manuel and Matheus Vicente and is a fine example of Portuguese Baroque. In the north of Portugal, Niccolo Nazzoni was developing his own Baroque style and he was particularly active in Porto where the Church of dos Clerigos (1732-48) exemplifies his genius for endowing the heavy granite of which Porto is largely built with a lightness and suppleness that is a delight to the eye.

In 1755 Lisboa was largely destroyed by an earthquake which killed some 30-40,000 people and ruined 300 palaces and 100 churches. Fortunately, the Marquês de Pombal was entrusted with the rebuilding of the city, which owes its fine central layout, open squares and impressive municipal buildings to his own vision and determination. Indeed, Lisboa is one of the most beautiful cities of the world and gives some idea of what the city of London might have looked like if Wren had been allowed to put his plans into execution after the Great Fire. Note particularly the arcades round the Praça do Comércio which were designed by Santos de Carvalho. Other fine buildings of this period are the Church of Nossa Senhora de Conceição Velha, the Basilica de Estrela (1779-90) with its luxuriant interior decorations (both in Lisboa) and the New Cathedral in Coimbra with its gorgeous façade.

Since the late 18th century little of value has been designed, but many old buildings which were pillaged or destroyed by Napoleon's marauding soldiers have been restored or rebuilt. Now, however, new blocks of flats, hospitals and schools are going up which reflect an intelligent use of modern materials in keeping with the refound confidence and individuality of the Portuguese.

Literature

The literature of Portugal has inevitably been closely linked with that of Spain—many Portuguese poets wrote in both Castilian and Portuguese—and was influenced at an early stage by the Provençal courtly writers and the troubadours of northern France. Prior to the 13th century, however, the most interesting type of writing and one that was certainly unique to Galicia and northern Portugal was the *cossante,* a brief, repetitive poem recalling oriental forms and characterised by *saudade,* a wistful melancholy that forms a constant element in Portuguese literature. King Duarte (1433-38) analysed the term with great care, pointing out that it had no equivalent in any other language, is born of the senses rather than of reason and may be pleasurable or sad. It bears some resemblance to the blues—'If you haven't got them today, you'll have them tomorrow; that is always providing you didn't have them yesterday.'

In the 13th century, partly as a result of Afonso III's 13 years in France, partly through the pilgrims who came to Santiago de Campostella in Galicia, the dominant influence was Provençal and was to remain so till the 16th century, although there was always a native poetry which maintained its own impetus parallel with more literary forms. **King Diniz** (1279-1325), who founded Coimbra university, was one of the most learned men of his time and one of the best poets. His charming *cantigas de amigo* or songs in which a woman mourns her lover's absence have a strong Portuguese flavour and simplicity which contrasts favourably with later poetry which displays a rather sterile interest in forms and conceits.

At this time little prose was being written, although Diniz commissioned many translations from Spanish, Latin and Arabic. Prose was to come to the fore in the 15th century—the great age of discovery and expansion —with the creation of the office of Royal Chronicler (1434) of which the first and possibly the greatest exponent was **Fernão Lopez** (1380-1460). Unfortunately only three of his ten chronicles of the Kings of Portugal remain, but they demonstrate his ability to combine spontaneity with the scruples of an accurate historian and to be both exact and imaginative. His successor, **Gomez Eanez de Zurara** (c 1410-74) continued the chronicles, but his most important work is the *Chronicle of the Discovery and Conquest of Guinea* which celebrated the achievements of Henry the Navigator. Zurara became extremely wealthy and contrived to combine erudition with good living by being adopted by the widow of a successful furrier.

The most distinguished chronicler of the 16th century was **João de Barros** (?1496-1570) who, apart from writing a long chivalrous romance, produced in 1552 the first of three *Decadas* of a long work entitled *Asia*. This work was planned in 40 books and was to deal with the history of Portuguese growth from 1409-1539. It is remarkable for its objectivity and immense learning and includes fascinating chapters on Eastern cities and customs, locusts, chess and monsoons. The book was continued by **Diogo do Couto** (1542-1616) who was also a much-travelled historian and as much at home in the fields of commerce and arms as in his role of *Cronista Mor* of India. From his home in Goa he wrote nine further

Campinos or herdsmen

Decadas which suffered shipwreck, fire, theft and bureaucratic delays and were published only in very scrappy form.

Fernão Lopez de Castanheda (*c* 1500-59) also wrote a long *History of the Discovery and Conquest of India* (1551-54), making himself personally acquainted with the ground and with many of those who had played a part in the years following Vasco da Gama's landing. Described in an unassuming style, the great events and personalities, the capture of Goa or Diu, the characters of Gama or Albuquerque stand out all the more clearly for the deliberate exclusion of rhetoric. Finally, **Gaspar Correa** (*c* 1495- *c* 1565) who was a personal secretary to Afonso de Albuquerque and spent most of his life in India, wrote a history of India from 1497 to 1550 based on first-hand accounts by da Gama's sailors and on his own experience. He spared no pains to obtain information from aged officials, Moors, natives, a Christian galley-slave or Albuquerque himself whose account of the sack of Malacca has all the excitement of an eye-witness's story. Correa's concern for truth, accuracy and objectivity made him unpopular with many powerful men and probably led to his murder in Malacca.

It is clear that India inspired fine historical writing as, indeed, did the Americas, but the greatest work to come out of Portugal's fantastic oriental expansion was **Luis de Camões's** (?1524-1580) *Os Lusíadas* (1572). This tells of Vasco da Gama's voyage to India in 10 cantos and interwoven into the story are descriptions of all Portugal's overseas possessions and the history of the Portuguese or Lusitanians. The poem is the great national epic and is probably the finest of all Renaissance epics. It was written partly before Camões set out for India and was completed during 17 unhappy years in India, Malacca and Mozambique. The work is distinguished both by the great breadth and grasp of events that it displays and by the realism of its descriptions—a storm off the Cape of Good Hope, the first appearance of land, ships arriving with purple banners flying or setting out down the cool, green waters of the Tagus.

Camões was also a great lyric poet and lover of nature, writing in sonnets, odes and eclogues of the countryside of his beloved Portugal, of his love for Caterina de Athaide and of his wish to live a quiet life in the country where he could devote himself to poetry. He was born of a good family at either Coimbra or Lisboa, spent most of his life in poverty and died of the plague at Lisboa shortly before Philip II entered Portugal. It would have been of small consolation to him to know that he was one of the first men for whom Philip enquired on his entry into Lisboa.

Some time before Camões began writing there had been a lyric revival in Portugal which produced some outstanding writers. **Bernadim Ribeiro** (?1486-1552) wrote some hauntingly beautiful love poetry and his love for the Infanta Beatriz, daughter of Manoel I, was celebrated by the 19th-century writer **Almeida Garrett** in his drama *Um Auto de Gil Vicente*. **Garcia de Resende** who edited the *Cancioneiro Geral* (1516) and was one

of its most distinguished contributors is best known for his verses on the
death of Inès de Castro, a rich theme for Portuguese writers. **Francisco
de Sá de Miranda** (c 1485-1558) introduced new poetic forms to Portugal
from Italy and revived artificial classical comedy modelled on Terence.
Christovam Falcão (c 1512-1557) wrote delightful eclogues whose evoca-
tion of the dreamy charm of many regions of Portugal have been called
the last echo of the Provençal lute. **Gil Vicente** (c 1470-c 1540) was one
of the best poets of the language, second only to Camões, but his great
achievement and one that is almost unique in the history of Portuguese
literature was in the theatre.

It has been said that he was the founder of a national theatre which died
with its founder and certainly no one of note wrote anything for the
theatre again until the 19th century, although **Antonio Ferreira's** (1528-
1569) *Inès de Castro* has achieved a certain populari-
tion came from Spain, although he may have found the germs of his
inspiration in the dialogues of the early *cantigas de amigo,* and, of course,
in religious ritual and festivities. It was in Spain that he was to exercise
his greatest influence. Eleven of his 44 plays were written wholly in
Spanish and 17 partly, but the place of his birth is uncertain, although
it is likely that he came of poor parents who lived in the province of
Beira. In his trilogy of the *Barcas* he showed a talent for serious work,
but his forte was comedy and comic characterisation. During his time at
the court of Portugal he wrote plays which contain a host of well-
observed individuals and vivid comic scenes. He was also an accomplished
satirist and frequently inveighed against the corruption of the Church
and its representatives. His plays, however, often written in a hurry and
frequently almost improvised on the spot, were badly constructed and
this factor, as much as anything else, is responsible for the lack of plays
in the Portuguese.

During the 17th century Portugal suffered a political and consequently
a literary eclipse and little of value was written. Censorship was imposed
and education was in the hands of the Jesuits. The leading writer of the
age was **Francisco Manuel de Mello** (1608-66) who towards the end of his
life was able to say that it would be difficult to find an idle hour in it.
Born in Lisboa, he was a true aristocrat of literature, but he made many
enemies, spent 11 years in prison, was temporarily exiled to Brazil and
spent the last years of his life on important diplomatic missions to
London, Rome and Paris. He faced his misfortunes with a gaiety and
wisdom which is apparent in the wit and concision of his essays and
portraits of men and women in *Apologos Dialogaes.* He also wrote
a lively farce, *Auto de Fidalgo Aprendiz* (1646), but the court preferred
Italian opera, French plays and Spanish *zarzuelas* or musical comedies.
The most interesting work of the period was the *Lettres Portuguaises*
(Paris, 1669) which appeared in 1819 as *Cartas de uma Religiosa Portu-
gueza.* These were five love letters written in French by the nun **Marianna
Alcoforado** (1640-1723) to Colonel Nöel Bouton, Comte de Saint-

Portuguese peasants

Léger, immediately after he had deserted her. In their disorder, contradictions and barely repressed passion they bring a breath of life to the stilted writing of the day.

The 18th century saw several attempts to revive drama, but these were all deservedly unsuccessful and the most notable writings of this period were historical and scholarly works. Several academies or *arcadias* were founded which produced some outstanding critics and attempts were made to liberalise all branches of letters. This impulse was to culminate in Romanticism which, stemming from Germany, swept through England and France to find ready acceptance in Portugal. During the first half of the 19th century Portugal was seething with violence and unrest and returning exiles from England and elsewhere brought fresh ideas to the country. **Almeida Garrett,** who had spent some time at Hackney, not only re-invigorated drama but also introduced elements of fervent, natural beauty to his fellow-countrymen in the epics *Camões* (1825) and *Dona Branca* (1826). He was born in Porto in 1799 and died in 1854 after a life of writing and activity in all kinds of governmental posts. **Antonio Feliciano de Castilho** (1800-75), an altogether serener figure, sought his inspiration in the bucolic writings of Bernadim Ribeiro and other poets of the 15th and 16th centuries.

The reaction against Romanticism was lead by **Anthero de Quental** (1842-91) who studied law at Coimbra and was a student of German philosophy and poetry. In his *Odes Modernas* (1865) and *Sonetos* (1881) we have the rare spectacle of a Portuguese poet who tried not merely to express his own feelings nor to create some imprecise and attractive impression but to express the truth through poetry. A tortured and sincere man whose life, paradoxically, had all the trappings of the romantic, he shot himself in the square of his birthplace in the Azores, Ponta Delgada.

Throughout the 19th century Portuguese literature was rich in novelists and poets and this is no less true today. **Herculano** (1810-77) was inspired by the Waverley novels during his exile and launched the historical romance with *O Monástico* (1844-48), a novel in two parts which was based on scrupulous historical research. **Camillo Castelo Branco** (1825-90) portrayed the domestic and social scene with humour and charm even though his writing is sometime rather unbalanced and discursive. The *Só* (1892) of **António Nobre** (1867-1900) is a collection of poems of suffering and disillusion, shot through with exotic visions and tranquil simplicity, which with their all-pervading *saudade* are still extremely widely read.

Today Portugal has several good novelists and outstanding poets such as **José Regio** and **Miguel Torga,** but she is strongest in the fields of literary criticism and history for, as in the 15th and 16th century, the strength of Portuguese letters lies in its search for the truth.

Painting and Sculpture

The Portuguese genius expressed itself most effectively in the fields of architecture and literature and she produced no sculptors of note, although in the 16th century there was a school at Belém which was strongly influenced by French and Flemish art.

In painting the greatest Portuguese artist was **Nuno Gonçalves** whose 15th-century polyptych for the Church of São Vicente in Lisboa (now in the museum) depicting the famous and infamous, the princes and peasants of Portugal's Golden Age is fit to rank with the masterpieces of Giovanni Bellini or Giorgione. This work heralded the brief appearance of a school of Portuguese painters and portraitists of whom the most successful was **Vasco Fernandes.** His work can best be studied at Viseu and examples of the work of other 16th-century artists can be seen at Lisboa and Coimbra. In the 18th century **Domingos Vieira** painted some arresting portraits which can be seen at the museum in Lisboa.

THE PORTUGUESE LANGUAGE

Portuguese is spoken rapidly, with much slurring of unstressed syllables, linking together of words, and assimilation of sounds. Its complicated pronunciation makes it a most difficult language to master. Although the tourist will find little difficulty in reading Portuguese, he will find it very difficult to understand what is said to him.

No transcription into English symbols can represent with complete accuracy the complexity and nuances of Portuguese sounds. A single letter may have different sounds, depending on its position within the word and on its relation to other letters. However, phrasebooks and dictionaries should be helpful.

HOW TO GET THERE

NOTE. *American and Canadian tourists may find the following information useful if they choose one of the United Kingdom countries as the first step on their European itinerary.*

By Air. BEA, TAP and BUA run regular flights direct from London to Lisboa. Other airlines including BOAC and VARIG also have services as part of longer trans-continental flights. Tourist return £60 ($168). Mid-week Night Tourist £40 ($112) return. Flying time is 2 hrs 35 min.

BEA and TAP also run flights to Porto with bus connections to the northern coastal resorts. Fares: Tourist return £56 ($156). Mid-week Night Tourist £36 ($100) return. Baggage allowances are 44 lb Tourist Class, 66 lb First Class. Flying time is just over 2 hrs.

The new airport at Faro in the Algarve is now open. Tourist return £62 ($174). Mid-week Night Tourist £43 ($120) return. There are also connections between Lisboa and Faro by chauffeur-driven car, or by train which takes 5-7½ hours, according to your destination. Alternatively, you can fly to Gibraltar at a cost of £57 ($159) return Day Tourist or £35 ($98) return Mid-week Night Tourist. It is possible to rent a car in Gibraltar through BEA or Hertz and drive to the Algarve via Cadiz, Sevilla, Huelva, Ayamonte and Vila Real de Santo Antonio. The drive takes between 6 and 8 hours according to stops.

By Sea. By far the most attractive way of reaching Lisboa is by sea. Unfortunately, sailings are such that it is rarely possible to get bookings to coincide with a two or three weeks' holiday. Companies operating services calling at Lisboa include the Royal Mail Line, P & O Lines, Blue Star Line, Currie Line and Grimaldi Siosa. Fares vary from £28 to £32 ($78-89) first class, £20 to £22 ($56-61) second class and £18 to £22 ($50-61) tourist class. Return fares are double the single fare, less 10 per cent.

Klosters Sunward ferries operate a weekly car-ferry service from Southampton to Vigo (Spain) and Lisboa.

By Rail. This is the cheapest method of getting to Portugal although extremely tiring. For just under £31 ($86) return it is possible to travel by rail to Newhaven, steamer to Dieppe and thence by rail via Paris, Hendaye, Medina del Campo, Fuentes de Oñoro, Pampilhosa and Entroncamento to Lisboa. This involves second class travel through France and Portugal and third class travel in Spain, totalling some 50 hours.

Sargaceiro with a net used for gathering seaweed

The quickest route by rail involves first class travel throughout and takes just over 40 hrs to Lisboa. Passengers take the London-Paris night ferry via Dover and Dunkirk and the Sud Express from Paris (Austerlitz) to Irún on the Franco/Spanish border. The journey is completed on the Spanish/Portuguese Sud Express and you will have to change at the border as a different gauge is used on the railways in the Iberian Peninsula. Fares vary considerably but are round about £40 ($112) return. Meals, porters and other incidentals add to the total cost.

By Road. Unless you are going on a bus tour with perhaps a week's stay at a single resort, travel to Portugal by road is rather exhausting and can take up to four days reasonable driving from Calais to Lisboa (1,271 miles). This is a large slice out of even a three-week holiday, but your best route is by car-ferry from Southampton to Le Havre (daily sailings at 15.30 and 23.00 hrs) and thence over the Seine by the new Tancarville suspension bridge on road nos. 810 and 834 to Bernay where you join the 138 to Alençon and Le Mans. At Le Mans take the 158 to Tours where you join the E3 which will bring you to the Spanish border at Irún. This road will eventually take you right through to Coimbra and Lisboa for the central and southern Portuguese resorts. For the northern resorts you should take the E50 just after San Sebastian along the northern Spanish coast and then cut down via Lugo and Orense, crossing the Portuguese frontier at Valença or Vila Verde. An International Driving Permit, obtainable from the A.A.A. ($3), A.A. or R.A.C. (10/6), is essential for crossing Spain.

If you want to have your car in Portugal for touring without the effort of driving it there, you can fly it to Le Touquet or Calais, drive to Paris and take a car-sleeper express to Biarritz where you can continue on the E3. There is also a car-ferry service from Newhaven to Dieppe which connects with the Dieppe-Biarritz car-sleeper. These expresses run three or four times a week in summer and full details of all services can be obtained from the A.A., the R.A.C. or the Car-Ferry Centre, 52 Grosvenor Gardens, London, S.W.1.

Inclusive Air Holidays. Several U.K. tour operators are now running excellent inclusive air holidays to the North, Lisboa and the Algarve. The overall cost of these holidays is often little more than that of the scheduled flight.

CLIMATE

Portugal is wedge shaped, sloping from the high central massif of the Iberian Peninsula in the east down to the Atlantic Ocean in the west. The influence of the Atlantic protects the country from the extremes of temperature prevailing further inland. Sunshine averages are high, but even with very high temperatures in August, there is nearly always a cool breeze to take the edge off the heat. Rainfall is fairly evenly spread throughout the year, and consequently the vegetation is always green.

Portugal can be divided into three geographical regions. First, the northern area consisting of the Minho and Douro areas reached from Porto. Here the autumn, winter and spring months are cool and rainfall is heaviest in the period from October to May. During June, July, August and September the weather is perfect with blue skies and nearly constant sunshine.

Average rainfall and temperatures (Fahrenheit) for the northern area.

Month	Max	Min	Rainfall in inches	Sea temp
January	56	40	6·1	56
February	58	41	4·8	56
March	61	45	5·4	57
April	64	48	4·0	58
May	66	51	3·2	59
June	73	56	1·6	60
July	76	58	·8	61
August	77	58	·7	61
September	75	56	2·5	63
October	69	51	4·2	61
November	61	46	5·1	58
December	56	41	6·5	57

The second region is Central Portugal, being the Lisboa and Estoril area and resorts reached from the capital. Here the main characteristics are an even climate with long periods of sunshine and a low but evenly spread rainfall over the winter months. The central area is ideal for most tourists, as it is rarely unbearably hot and practically never really cold. Sea temperatures are not up to Mediterranean standards, but the water is appreciably warmer than in north-western Europe.

Average rainfall and temperatures (Fahrenheit) for the central area.

Month	Max	Min	Rainfall in inches	Sea temp
January	59	47	2·7	56
February	61	49	2·2	56
March	63	51	1·5	57
April	67	52	1·2	58
May	70	56	1·8	59
June	74	59	·3	60
July	79	62	·0	62
August	79	63	·4	62
September	77	62	·8	63
October	72	57	1·1	61
November	65	51	2·8	59
December	59	48	4·1	57

The third region is the southern area known as the Algarve. This part of Portugal includes the coastline facing south and extending from the Spanish border in the east to Sagres in the west. Its main characteristics are even temperatures with long periods of sunshine, low humidity and practically no rain during the summer months.

A beautiful area at any time, the Algarve is particularly lovely in springtime when the almonds are in blossom. It is becoming a very popular coast for Easter, Whitsun and Autumn visits, and it is often possible to swim at Christmas.

Average rainfall and temperatures (Fahrenheit) for the southern area.

Month	Max	Min	Rainfall in inches	Sea temp
January	67	53	1·4	62
February	68	54	2·5	64
March	69	55	2·1	68
April	75	57	1·0	69
May	81	63	·9	72
June	85	68	·1	74
July	92	72	·0	77
August	95	73	·0	80
September	90	72	·0	80
October	82	61	1·3	74
November	74	58	2·4	70
December	67	51	1·9	65

Algarve chimneys

HOTELS IN PORTUGAL

Until comparatively recently, there was a distinct shortage of hotel accommodation in Portugal. Even now, it is not safe to assume that small inland towns will have tourist class hotels without first checking. The Government Department which controls hotel prices, the *Comissariado do Turismo* (C.D.T.) is filling in all the gaps as fast as possible and many new hotels have been completed in the past few years. Foreign capital is also being used to build hotels, particularly in the Algarve.

As in Spain, every hotel in Portugal has its official classification—Luxury, Class I, Class II and Class III. Prices are fixed according to the category and cases of over-charging are rare. In the unlikely event of this happening, send your bill with a covering letter to the nearest office of C.D.T.

Apart from hotels, there are three other types of accommodation.

Pousadas [poh-zah′dås]: These are small inns designed primarily for motorists and controlled by the C.D.T. They are essentially Portuguese in character, architecture, furnishings and food. They are always clean, comfortable, simple and good. Their prices are very reasonable, and bookings should be made well in advance. Theoretically, at any rate, one is limited to a stay of five days.

Estalagens [ish-tå-lah′zhen]: These are independently operated inns, tending to be more expensive than *pousadas*. Some are very good indeed, others can leave a lot to be desired. I have found that their classification is not always an indication of standard.

Pensões [pen-sown′]: *A pensão* is of a lower grade than the three other types of accommodation. It roughly approximates to a private hotel or boarding house. Some are excellent, but others may have rather primitive plumbing.

Most hotels will quote bed-and-breakfast or demi-pension rates, but in *pensões* and *estalagens* it is usual to take full pension. To all hotel bills is added 10 per cent service charge and a 3 per cent local tax in resorts. Tipping should therefore be on a modest scale and for services rendered.

The C.D.T. publish an excellent list of *Hotels, Pousadas, Estalagens* and *Pensões*. It is available on application to the Casa de Portugal, 20 Lower Regent Street, London, S.W.1, or Casa de Portugal, 570 Fifth Avenue, New York 10036.

In Portuguese hotels, afternoon tea, as we know it, is virtually unknown. The following meals will be provided:

Breakfast: *pequeno almoço* (pe-kay'noo al-moh'soo). This is always of the abbreviated continental variety and consists of coffee, rolls, butter and, possibly, jam. In larger hotels you can obtain cooked dishes by paying a supplement.

Lunch: *almoço* [al-moh'soo].

Dinner: *jantar* [zhan-tar'].

For food and wine see pages 30-5.

In common with many continental countries, very few hotels provide soap in bedrooms, so it is wise to take your own. Except in larger establishments, it is unusual to have your shoes cleaned by the hotel. You will find a shoe-black in every café.

AVERAGE HOTEL PRICES PER PERSON PER DAY		
	single room	double room
	esc	esc
Luxury	190	350
Class 1 a	140	200
Class 1 b	100	150
Class 2	90	120
Class 3	70	110
Pensão 1	50	90

See **Currency,** page 35.

EATING IN PORTUGAL

Portuguese cooking is related to Spanish, but has overtones of French. Yet the use of Portuguese oil, tomatoes and fish manage to produce a cuisine that is distinctive to the country. Catering in tourist class hotels, *pousadas, estalagens* and the higher category *pensões* will be found abundant and acceptable to foreign palates. The lower categories of *pensões* and cheap restaurants tend to use a quality of oil that is offensive to most tourists.

Portuguese fish is excellent and comes in a bewildering range of shapes, sizes and colours. Paradoxically, with all this fresh fish to be had for the catching, the national dish is dried cod (*bacalhau*), which is reputed to be cooked in over a hundred different ways. Another dish peculiar to Portugal, and one that every visitor should try, is *caldo verde, a* potato, cabbage and sausage soup. Fruit is plentiful, cheap and of excellent quality. Most visitors prefer to take fruit in place of the endless sticky concoctions of sugar and egg yolk, of which the Portuguese are so fond.

Here are a few of the dishes you are most likely to meet:

Soup (*caldo, sopa*).

Caldo Verde.	See above. Stop the waiter before he pours spoonfuls of olive oil on it. This is a local habit that doesn't always agree with other constitutions.
Caldeirada.	Fish soup with onions. Very good if you like this sort of thing.
Canja.	Chicken soup with rice.
Ensopada.	Rich meat soup with bread.

Hors d'Oeuvres (*acepipes*).
Usually excellent. Contents consist of all or some of the following: Olives, hard boiled eggs, tunny-fish, sardines, mussels, tomato, potato salad, fish cakes made of *bacalhau*.

Fish (*peixe*).

Ameijoas.	A small shellfish which is much nicer to eat than it looks. They are sometimes served with *hors d'oeuvres*. They are also cooked like mussels, served with croquettes or used as a garnish with pork.
Atum.	Tunny-fish. Delicious grilled or cold with mayonnaise.
Bacalhau.	Dried cod (*see* above). It is delicious when cooked in one of the hundred or so ways, but don't look at it hanging up in a shop. You'd never eat it!
Camarões.	Shrimps.
Chocos.	Cuttlefish.
Eiros.	Eels.
Gambas.	Prawns.
Lagosta.	Crayfish.
Lagostinhas.	Dublin Bay Prawns. Usually eaten cold with mayonnaise.
Lampreia.	Lamprey. Very good indeed. Speciality of the Minho.
Linguado.	Sole. They are as good as the finest Dover Soles and are cooked and garnished with loving care.
Lulas.	Squid.
Mexilhões.	Mussels.
Ostras.	Oysters. These are not the oysters we know as Portuguese. Although some people rave about them, I find them too large and tasteless.

Harvest-time in the vineyards

Pregado.	Turbot. Beautiful quality fish, but too often unexcitingly prepared.
Pescada.	Usually hake, but sometimes cod is served under this name. Again, the preparation is often unimaginative.
Salmão.	Salmon. Best in the Minho region whence it comes. Expensive.
Salmonete.	Red mullet. Excellent. The best is to be found at Cascais.
Sardinhas.	More often served grilled fresh, when they are particularly good. Of the tinned variety, try those flavoured with lemon.

Meat (*carne*).	
Anho.	Lamb. Not favoured by the Portuguese.
Bife.	This is the main dish of a meal in most households that can afford it. Sometimes very good, it often tends to be tough and tasteless. Beef served in any other way than steak is rare.
Bife de Vitela.	Veal. Often good.
Cabrito.	Kid. Usually very good indeed.
Carne de Porco.	Pork. Often eaten in stews with shellfish, which is much nicer than it sounds.
Leitão.	Suckling pig. Excellent roast with all the trimmings, it is also good cold.
Presunto.	Superb smoked hams from Trás-os-Montes and the Minho; similar to Italian *prosciutto*.

Tripas.	Tripe. This is a very popular dish and usually of high quality.

Vegetables (*vegetal, verdura, hortaliça*).

Alcachofras.	Artichokes.
Alface.	Lettuce.
Batata.	Potato.
Couve Galega.	Cabbage.
Espargos.	Asparagus.
Espinafres.	Spinach.
Favas.	Broad Beans.
Feijao.	Beans, often made into a sort of stew.
Nabos.	Turnips.
Pepino.	Cucumber.
Salada.	Salad.

Fruit (*fruta*).

Ameixas.	Plums.
Cerejas.	Cherries.
Damasco.	Apricot.
Figos.	Figs.
Laranja.	Orange.
Limão.	Lemon.
Maçã.	Apple.
Morangos.	Strawberries. These have a long season in Portugal, are cheap and very good.
Pera.	Pear.
Pessego.	Peach.
Uvas.	Grapes.

Dessert (*sobremesa*).

There are dozens of sweets in Portugal made from combinations of sugar, egg yolks and almond paste. They go under a great variety of names. To me, at any rate, they all taste the same—sweet and cloying.

Doces de Amendoa.	
Doce d'ovos.	
Ovos Moles.	See above.
Palha.	
Queijos do Céu.	
Pudim Flã.	Caramel Cream.
Queijadas de Sintra.	Cheese cakes.

Cheese (*queijo*).

Portuguese cheeses are extremely good with the exception of the imitation 'Dutch' variety.

Azeitão.	A soft white cheese which you can decapitate and eat with a spoon. Best in Lisbon as it comes from nearby Azeitão.
Serra.	A yellow cheese in top condition when it is slightly soft.
Rabacal.	Delicious goat's cheese.
Queijo Fresco.	White cream cheese.

WHAT TO DRINK IN PORTUGAL

Water. Tap water is safe in Lisboa, Estoril, Porto, and in most large tourist resorts. Even so, to be on the safe side, anybody with a delicate stomach, or young children, should stick to one of the excellent cheap mineral waters.
Pedras Salgadas (fizzy).
Vidago (slightly fizzy).
Luso (flat).

Coffee (*café*). Portuguese coffee (mostly Brazilian) is among the best in the world. The locals drink theirs very strong and sweet. If you want it white, ask for *Café com leite.*

Tea (*cha*). This is mostly of the tea-bag variety and drunk with lemon. In larger hotels and cafés they now are used to serving it with milk (*com leite*).

Wine (*vinho*). Portuguese wine, with the exception of port, is always palatable, goes with the food, but is rarely distinguished. It is for this reason that it is far better to drink the open wine of the house than to try to choose a particular kind. Portuguese law decrees that hotels etc. must offer their guests taking fixed price meals 3/5 of a litre of their house wine. You only have to ask for it.

Vinho branco.	White wine.
Vinho de Mesa.	Table wine of the house.
Vinho do Porto.	Port.
Vinho da região.	Wine from the locality.
Vinho Rosé.	Vin rosé.
Vinho tinto.	Red wine.
Vinho verde.	The *verde* means green in the sense of young. You can get *vinho verde* white, rosé and even red. The red is slightly sparkling, a great thirst quencher and the only red wine I know to be served on ice. These wines all come from the north, and, not being good travellers, are best drunk in their own region.

Wine boats on the Douro

Spirits. Imported whisky, gin and brandy are expensive, especially in hotel bars. The local gin, however, is quite acceptable in cocktails. The best brand is *Pheyses*. The local brandy, while making no pretence to be cognac, is a very palatable drink, both as a liqueur and as a long drink with ice and soda. Best brands are *Borges* and *Constantino*. Beware of some fire-water known as *Aguardente Bagaçeira*. This is a type of raw white brandy drunk mostly by the peasants at vintage time. There are several good local liqueurs, among which I particularly like *Triplice*.

Beer and Soft Drinks. Portuguese beer is of the continental light lager type and quite acceptable. It is available both in bottles and draught and is usually served ice-cold accompanied by a little saucer of nuts. *Sagres* is one of the most popular brands. A Portuguese version of Coca-Cola is found everywhere, and fresh lemon and orange juice are available.

And, of course, Port. Portuguese themselves drink little Port; that which they consume, as an apéritif, is of the dry white type. Although the vines that produce Port have grown in Portugal since the time of the Crusades, it was not until 1678 that Port as it is known today appeared. Two English wine merchants, after purchasing the entire output of a monastery vineyard, added some brandy to each of the casks to ensure that the produce would reach Britain in perfect condition. So popular did this become, that in 1703 Britain negotiated a trade treaty ensuring a virtual monopoly of port exports. Unhappily, the trade became so profitable that by the 19th century almost any fortified wine was being sold as the genuine article.

Nowadays, the Port Wine Institute controls the trade, and nothing can be sold as port which does not come from a strictly defined area of the

Douro Valley. Each shipment which comes down the river to Porto is examined by experts for colour, bouquet and quality. Every now and again in a particularly good year the wine will be declared a vintage. It is then bottled without blending and left to age in the bottles for years. A fine vintage port reaches its peak at 25 to 30 years old.

FACTS AND FIGURES

Currency. The unit is called an *escudo* [ish-koo'doo] (abbreviated to esc hereafter), which is divided into one hundred *centavos* [sen-tah'voos]. There are notes for 1,000, 500, 100, 50 and 20 esc; silver coins for 20, 10, 5 and 2½ esc; nickel coins for 1 esc and 50 centavos; and copper coins for 20 and 10 centavos. The Portuguese currency is a 'hard' one and there is no improving on the official rate of about 80 esc to the pound sterling; 29 to the U.S. dollar. Threepence per esc makes calculations fairly easy for U.K. tourists; 4 cents per esc for Americans.

Now and again, particularly from older people in country districts you will hear reference to *milreis* and *stoins*. These are out-dated and you should ask for the price in esc. 1,000 esc is sometimes called a *conto*, but this is normally used only in commercial transactions.

It is advisable to take most of your money in the form of Traveller's Cheques which are available from all banks and the leading travel agents. They come in suitable units of pounds and dollars, are changeable at all banks and the larger hotels; if you lose them, it is relatively easy to be supplied with more cheques if you are able to give details of their numbers to your bank. You should make a note of the numbers when you buy them and keep this separate from the cheques. You will have to bring your passport with you when buying the cheques and you should sign the top line on purchase. Do *not* sign the bottom line until you are actually cashing the cheques.

Scottish travellers should remember that Scottish bank notes are not legal tender outside the U.K. and will not be accepted abroad. American travellers will find it convenient to have $50-100 in dollar bills for small or last-minute expenses during their trip.

Passports. Visitors to Portugal must have a valid passport. Application should be made to either: Clive House, Petty France, *London S.W.1*

or: India Buildings, Water Street, *Liverpool 2*

or: 14 Princes Square, *Glasgow C.1*

You will need two passport photographs, the cost is 30s. and the passport is valid for five years and renewable for a further five. It is also possible to travel on a British Visitor's Passport which can be obtained from any Labour Exchange for 7s. 6d. on presentation of two photographs and birth certificate. It is valid for one year only.

American citizens should apply in person at Passport Division, Department of State, in Washington, D.C., New York, Boston, Miami, Chicago, New Orleans, Los Angeles, San Francisco or Seattle. If it is not possible to appear at any of these offices, make personal application before the clerk of any U.S. District Court System. Take along two unretouched photos, $2\frac{1}{2}$ inches square (no Polaroid or machine photos), a witness who has known you for at least two years, unless you can produce some identification that has a physical description (a driver's licence will do), your birth certificate or old passport for identification, and $10 ($5 for renewal of old passport). Allow a week to 10 days for processing. A passport issued after September 15, 1959 is good for three years, with one renewal for two years permitted. A smallpox vaccination is required for return to the U.S.

Visas are required by Commonwealth visitors with the exception of Australians and Canadians, and Americans should check with their travel agent as regulations do vary.

Customs. On entering Portugal, in common with any other country, you may be required to open your luggage. You should declare any spirits or tobacco, and also your cigarette lighter as there is a small annual tax on them. You will find immigration formalities are cut to the minimum and there are no currency controls whatever.

On your return to Britain, the Customs normally allow tourists of British nationality to bring in the following dutiable items:

200 cigarettes or 50 cigars, one bottle of spirits, one bottle of wine, up to £5 worth of souvenirs, and a small bottle of perfume. It should be remembered that these are concessions and to exceed them makes you liable to pay duty on all the goods in your possession, not merely the excess.

U.S. Customs permit duty free $100 retail value of purchases, per person, 1 quart of liquor, per person over 21, and 100 cigars, per person regardless of age.

Health. As there is no reciprocal National Health agreement between Great Britain and Portugal, it is essential to take out an insurance policy covering you for accidents and medical expenses. Any travel agent will be pleased to issue a cover note and the costs are very reasonable. American tourists should check their medical insurance policies to be sure they are covered while outside the U.S.A.

Generally speaking, it is not wise for tourists to drink the water in Portugal outside large towns. There are excellent and reasonably priced mineral waters available. (See page 33.) Until one is used to the richer cooking, it is wise to eat lightly for the first few days. Avoid drinking spirits in the heat of the day, and remember that drinking large quantities of iced liquid whilst very hot is likely to cause trouble. It is far better to sip a hot drink. Beware of the sun, especially at mid-day. Take it in very small doses to start with.

The unaccustomed oil used in cookery sometimes gives rise to minor stomach trouble, which, though not serious, can be very annoying while on a trip. Preventatives for 'travellers' complaints', as well as remedies for it, should be part of your emergency supplies.

If you should need a doctor, the nearest British or American Embassy or Consulate will supply the address of an English-speaking one.

Clothes. Reference to the temperature charts on pages 26-7 will give you an indication of the sort of clothing you will require on your holiday. Most hotels have a quick and good laundry service. On the beaches, many of the more popular resorts have relaxed their 'no bikini' rule, but in out-of-the-way places it is advisable to stick to one-piece costumes for women and shorts for men. Women in shorts are definitely frowned on off the beach, and even slacks will cause astonishment, if not disapproval in country places. Remember that when entering a church women should cover their heads and both sexes should wear a top with sleeves.

Smoking. British cigarettes and pipe tobacco are widely available in the main tourist areas at prices lower than those in Britain. This is due to the lower taxes in Portugal. Even so, it is worth bringing in your duty-free allowance if you are arriving by air as most British cigarettes obtainable on the continent are manufactured there under licence and are rarely as good as the British product. American cigarettes are readily available, and at the popular price. Cigars, too, are cheap, Havanas and Brazilian varieties being on sale. The local cigarettes are about 4 esc for 20, but too strong for most foreign palates.

Electricity. Nearly everywhere electricity is 210-220 volts A.C., but you may encounter 110-120 volts D.C. from time to time, so take your electric razor adaptor.

Tipping. I find that this is a subject that worries most tourists. In Portugal tipping in the hotels offers few difficulties. Every hotel automatically adds a 10 per cent service charge. It is, therefore, quite sufficient if you tip nominal sums to cover special services rendered. I normally leave about 20 esc for the chambermaid, with a similar amount for the waiter and hall-porter, for a stay of a fortnight. Five esc is enough for the man who takes your suitcases to your room. Taxi drivers should be tipped between 10 and 12 per cent of the fare shown on the meter. Porters at stations should be given 2½ esc per piece of luggage. Usherettes at theatres and cinemas 1 esc. Attendants at toilets in stations, cafés, hotels etc., 1 esc. On no account tip any airline staff.

If travelling by sea, take five per cent of the passage money and divide it between cabin steward, dining-room steward, deck steward and bath-room steward (if you have one), according to services rendered. Bar steward and wine steward you tip as you go.

In cafés charges are usually added to the bill. If so, leave any small change. Where service charges are not included, add 10 to 15 per cent.

The Praça do Império with adjoining Mosteiro dos Jerónimos, Lisboa

Shops and Banks. Shops in general open from about 9 a.m. to 1 p.m., and from 3 or 4 p.m. to about 7 p.m. Banks are usually open from 10 a.m. to noon, and from 2 p.m. to 4 p.m.

Post and Telephone. You can buy stamps from post offices only. Airmail to Britain is 3 esc 50 for letters, and 2 esc 50 for postcards; airmail to the U.S.A. is 4 esc 50 for letters, and 3 esc 30 for postcards. Letter boxes are red. Public telephone kiosks are painted red. Telephones are automatic. There are few English-speaking operators.

Toilet Facilities. Public lavatories are few and far between in Portugal. It is usual for tourists to make use of the facilities provided by hotels and cafés. You should tip the attendant 1 esc or 50 centavos. Lavatories are called W.C. or *lavabo,* and will be marked *Cavalheiros* [kå-vå-lyay'ee-roosh], or *Homens* [o'mensh] for men and *Senhoras* [se-nyoh'råsh] for women.

TRANSPORTATION

Air. There is a daily flight from Lisboa to Porto and return. The new airport at Faro is now open and TAP operates flights three times a week to and from Lisboa. TAP also provides flights to Madeira.

Trains. There is an excellent, cheap and frequent service of electric trains running from the Cais do Sodré terminus in Lisboa to Estoril and Cascais. Main line trains are on the whole fast, good and punctual. There are two classes, and most foreign tourists travel first class. From Lisboa to Porto takes about 4 hrs. From Lisboa to the Algarve about 6 hrs, and from Lisboa to Coimbra about 3 hrs. Even on a short journey individual seats are allocated to travellers. It is therefore important to make your reservations in ample time.

Buses. There is a good network of bus services which are cheap, but in country districts often crowded and infrequent. Several agencies also organise excellent excursions.

Taxis. Taxis are plentiful in the main centres and are cheap. There are two kinds: 4-seaters and 6-seaters, and the rates are different. However, the charges are plainly posted and all cabs are metered. You are entitled to two minutes free waiting for every kilometer on the clock. There is no extra charge at night, but there is a 50 per cent surcharge for baggage weighing over 60 lb. Should you hire a taxi for an out-of-town trip, the driver is entitled to be paid the return fare or quote a flat rate.

Car Rental. TAP and BEA can both offer facilities in Portugal. Hertz and Avis also have agencies. R.M. Carreras Lda. of Lisboa, whose staff all speak English, have a range of new British and Continental models available. A small four-seater would cost about £28 ($78) for a fortnight, including insurance.

Renters need either a valid national driving licence or an International Driving Licence. The latter is imperative if you intend to cross the border into Spain, and you are recommended to acquire one.

Lisboa Public Transport. There are two underground railway lines (*Metropolitano*) in Lisboa. Fixed fare is 1 esc 50. In addition, there is a good system of buses, trams and funicular trams. Ferry boats leave for Cacilhas from the Praça do Comércio; for Barreiro and Alcochete from the Estacão do Sul e Sudeste; for Trafaria from the Estacão Fluvial de Belém.

Police. Police wear a pale grey uniform and a peak cap. Tourist police, who normally speak a little English, can be distinguished by their red armbands. Lisboa police take a very poor view of 'jay-walking'. You should make a special point of observing traffic lights and police signals when exploring the city on foot.

IF YOU ARE MOTORING

If you are taking a car into Portugal you will require these documents: green insurance (liability) card, registration book and driving licence. If entering through Spain you will need an International Driving Licence. You also need a triangular red reflector sign, similar to those required in Italy, for use if you stop at night, or in a bad position. These can be hired for 85 esc at Valença (E50), Vilar Formoso (E3) or Caia (E4) at the border or from the Automóvel Club de Portugal's offices in Lisboa or Porto. If the sign is returned in good condition with the receipt, the sum will be refunded, but these triangles are extremely useful in any country.

You may enter Portugal by any of the following frontier posts: Valença (Minho), Vila Verde da Raia and Quintanilha (Trás-os-Montes), Vilar Formoso and Segura (Beira), Galegos, Caia, S. Leonardo and Vila Verde de Ficalho (Alentejo), Vila Real de Santo António (Algarve).

The motoring organisation in Portugal, the Automobile Club of Portugal, will give advice and assistance to overseas motorists. It is advisable to take your A.A.A., A.A. or R.A.C. membership card with you. The A.C.P.'s regional addresses are as follows: Lisboa: 24 Rua Rosa Araújo; Porto: 2 Rua Gonçalo Cristóvão; Coimbra: 6 Avenida Navarro; Évora: 26 Praça do Geraldo.

In Portugal the International Convention road signs are used. You drive on the right and pass on the left. When passing use your horn and indicate you are about to pass. It is usual to indicate that you are returning to your side of the road after passing. Use of the horn in Lisboa or Porto is strictly forbidden. Traffic lights are an amber caution light, red stop light and green for go. A green light on the right indicates that you may turn right even when the red light ahead is against you.

indicates that you may turn right even when the red light ahead is against you.

In common with all European countries, vehicles coming from the right have priority unless otherwise indicated by traffic signs.

There is no speed limit on the open road, but in built-up areas it is forbidden to exceed 60 km per hour.

Parking is available in most towns and cities, costing from 1 esc 50 to 2 esc 50 per day in public car parks. You may also park at the curb-side, except where a No Parking sign is displayed. (No Parking and two arrows pointing towards each other.) In some places there is parking on different sides of the street on alternate days. Parking is not allowed less than 5 metres from bends, 3 metres from tram stops and 10 metres from bus stops.

Lisboa is a difficult city for a stranger to drive in, and if you take my advice, you will leave your car in the car park and use taxis or public transport.

The main roads in Portugal are well sign-posted, have good surfaces and are delightfully free of traffic. Garages carry the usual well-known brands of fuel. Regular Grade costs 23 esc per gallon and Premium Grade 27 esc per gallon. In some of the country districts filling stations are few and far between, and it is wise to carry some fuel in reserve.

Tire Pressures

Lb per sq in	22	23	24	25	26	27	28
Kg per sq cent	1.54	1.61	1.68	1.75	1.83	1.90	1.96

CAMPING

Camping sites in Portugal have not reached the heights of sophistication of those in France and Spain Nevertheless, there are nearly a hundred recognised sites. Campers should be in possession of a 'Carta de Campista' for Portugal or apply through their local clubs for an International Camping Card. The address of the *Federação Portugesa de Campismo* is: Rua da Madalena, 75-2, Lisboa. The Orbitur Company, Av. Almirante Gago Coutinho 439, Lisboa has some 25 sites and also bungalows with cooking facilities. The government owned sites are equipped with swimming pools.

Caravan or travel-trailer owners should observe the following speed limits: on the open road 60 kph; in built-up areas, 40 kph.

The following are a few of the camp sites situated on or near beaches:

Viana do Castelo. (Praia do Cabedelo.)
Ofir. (Pine woods near bank of River Cávado.)
Esposende. (Near the town.)

Aveiro. (Costa Nova pine woods.)
Figueira da Foz. (Serra da Boa Viagem.)
S. Pedro de Muel. (Pine woods near sea.)
Nazaré. (Parque das Pedralvas.)
S. Martinho do Porto. (Pine woods on south side of beach.)
Peniche. (Near the town.)
Berlenga Islands. (Information from Tourist Office, Peniche.)
Sesimbra. (Fonte de Cavalo.)
Setúbal. (Parque de Comenda.)
Sines. (Pine woods near sea.)
Vila Nova de Milfontes. (Pine woods near sea.)
Lagos. (Near lighthouse.)
Vila Real de Santo António. (Pine woods.)
Monte Gordo. (Pine woods by beach.)

There are also two sites near Lisboa belonging to the *Clube de Campismo de Lisboa*. Rua da Miserícordia 137-2°.

YOUTH HOSTELS, WORK CAMPS
AND HOLIDAY COURSES

There are a number of voluntary work camps which accept visitors from overseas. The age limits are 18 to 25 years. No pay or travel allowances, but free board and lodging are supplied. Apply to: *Organização Nacional da Mocidade Portuguesa,* Servico de Intercambio, Palácio da Independência, Lisboa.

Y.M.C.A. accommodation: Apply A.N.A.C.M., Rua de São Bento 329-2°, Lisboa.

There are a number of youth hostels in Portugal. Contact can be made through the Youth Hostels' Association. Hostels by the sea include those at Esposende, Sagres and Viana do Castelo. There is a hostel in Lisboa.

Academic Association of the Law Faculty of Lisboa University, Cidade Universitaria, Lisboa offers accommodation in its hostels and holiday centres in Lisboa and the neighbourhood. Prices are very reasonable.

Association of Students of the Advanced Technical Institute, Avenida Rovisco Pais, Lisboa arranges study groups and guided tours for foreign students during August. The association has holiday camps near Lisboa which are open from August to October and which can be used as centres for visiting the city.

Coimbra University runs summer courses every July and August for foreign students wanting to learn Portuguese. The course includes visits to the theatre and costs 400 esc with an additional 40 esc per day board and lodging.

Lisboa University also runs courses for foreign students in July and August. The course includes the language, literature and history of Portugal. The cost is about 500 esc, with board and lodging extra.

The National Foundation for Joy in Work, Calçada de Sant 'Ana 180, Lisboa, has holiday homes for young work-people which offer programmes including conferences, concerts and excursions. It also arranges exchanges between young workers in all countries.

The National Organisation of Portuguese Youth, Palácio da Independência, Largo de S. Domingos, Lisboa, welcomes young foreigners to its seaside and mountain centres during the summer. There is swimming, sailing and climbing, as well as an opportunity to meet young Portuguese people. Costs are very reasonable.

PUBLIC HOLIDAYS

The most important holidays in Portugal are:

January 1st (New Year); Good Friday; Easter Sunday; Corpus Christi; June 10th (National Day); August 15th (Assumption of Our Lady); October 5th (Proclamation of the Portuguese Republic); November 1st (All Saints' Day); December 1st (Independence Day); December 8th (Portugal's Patron-Saint Day); December 25th (Christmas Day).

In addition to these national holidays, there are various local feast days and festivals. During some of these the town or region concerned may well be either completely or partially on holiday. Consequently, if you are planning to arrive in a town during the local festival, it is wise to book accommodation well in advance and to ask whether restaurants, public buildings etc. will be open.

There are so many local festivals that it is impossible to give them all here. I have, however, listed the most important. Visitors should check the dates, as some of them vary slightly from year to year.

January	17	Santo Antão, *Alentejo*.
	20	São Sebastião, *Northern provinces*.
	22	São Vicente, *Northern provinces*.
February	2	Nossa Senhora da Luz, *Alentejo, Crato*.
April	23	São Jorge, *Penafiel*.
May	3	Festa da Cruzes, *Barcelos, Monsanto*
	12	Santa Joana, *Aveiro*.
	13	Nossa Senhora de Fátima, *Fátima*.
First Saturday in June		São Gonçalo, *Amarante*.
June	13/20	Santo Antonio, *Lisboa, Vila Real*.
	24	São João, *Lisboa, Fontainhas, Braga, Evora, Figueira da Foz, In Soberado* and *Valonga—Dance Festivals. Alentejo region—gypsy weddings*.
	29	São Pedro, *Lisboa, Vila Real*.
July	1	São Torquato, *Guimarães*.
	14/19	(Even years) Santa Isabel, *Coimbra*.
	7/8	Colete Encarnado, *Vila Franca de Xira*. (Bullfight Festival.)
	25	Sant'Iago, *Évora*.
August	4/6	Festas Gualterianas, *Guimarães*.
	10/15	Nossa Senhora da Abadia, *Amares, Bouro*.
	17	São Mamede, *Fontanelas*.
	17/19	Nossa Senhora da Agonia, *Viana do Castelo*.
	24	São Bartholomeu, *Serpa, Alentejo*.
October	13	Nossa Senhora de Fátima, *Fátima*.
November	11	São Martinho, *General*.

ENTERTAINMENT

Cinemas and Theatres. There are cinemas in all the main cities and towns. Performances are not continuous, the first showing being about 3 p.m. and the last at about 9.30 p.m. The films are mostly shown in their language of origin, and there are usually American and British films to be seen in the larger centres. One tips the usherette 1 esc.

There are a half-a-dozen or so theatres in Lisboa giving twice nightly performances of revue or music hall. As most of the acts are of a musical or visual nature, it is possible for tourists to enjoy them. These shows are not particularly sophisticated, but are good of their kind. Again, one tips the usherette.

There is a particularly beautiful theatre in Lisboa, the São Carlos Theatre, which from time to time has visiting foreign opera companies. It is obligatory to wear evening dress in the orchestra stalls and stage boxes on these occasions.

Night Life. Apart from the Casinos, many of the de luxe and first class hotels have dancing in the evenings. Conventional night clubs, as such, are few and far between except in Lisboa. In the capital there are half-a-dozen or so, all run along familiar lines and patronised almost exclusively by tourists.

Far more interesting are the *Adegas Tipicas,* little restaurants where you eat or drink while listening to the *fado. Fado* is the sad folk song peculiar to Lisboa. Its theme is nearly always unrequited love. Most of the *fado* restaurants are situated in the *Alfama* and *Bairro Alto* districts. One of them, *Viela,* belongs to the sister of the fabulous Amalia Rodrigues, who occasionally sings there. These little places are continuously changing, and it is therefore wiser to enquire on the spot as to which is currently the best. When last there, I went to *Lisboa à Noite* and found it excellent and reasonably priced. The address is 69 Rua das Gávèas.

Casinos. Apart from the casinos at Estoril, Espinho, Figueira da Foz and Póvoa de Varzim, which are licensed for gaming, 'casino' tends to be rather a misleading description. These establishments usually consist of a bridge room, dance hall, bar and restaurant. No gambling is permitted. In the licensed casinos the usual games of chance are roulette, baccarat and chemin de fer. You should take your passport with you to gain entrance.

Cafés. The café is the centre of life for a Portuguese man. It acts as 'pub', club, reading room, and often as place of business. The newspapers are available, a shoe-black in attendance, a telephone at hand, and always there is congenial company. Many cafés have an exclusively male clientèle, and visitors with women in their party should avoid giving offence by using this type. There will be another just around the corner where mixed company is acceptable. The Portuguese themselves drink little alcohol between meals. More often than not, they will be sipping a coffee or a mineral water over a game of chess or dominoes, Portuguese women rarely patronise the cafés. They have their own private preserve, the local tea shop. Here, over tea, lemonade, ice cream and pastries, they meet their friends to pass the time of day and exchange gossip.

SPORTING FACILITIES IN PORTUGAL

Skin Diving. The best underwater fishing area is undoubtedly the Algarve where water temperatures vary from 69° to 80° F during the season. Especially good is the stretch between Sagres and Lagos. Near Lisboa, Cascais makes a good centre, and on the south side of the Tagus Sesimbra, 32 km from Lisboa, has become a popular centre for the sport. Further north, the Berlenga Islands' *pousada* offers a very good base to explore the waters round about. In the summer there is a daily boat from Peniche.

Sailing. Estoril and Cascais are the main centres in Portugal for sailing. Regattas are held throughout the year, and principal events are for Dragons, Stars and twelve-metre Sharpies. Sailing is also to be had at Porto, Sesimbra and Figueira da Foz.

The *Federação Portuguesa de Vela* will give help and information to visiting yachtsmen.

Fresh Water Fishing. For fishing in the lakes, streams and rivers of Portugal a licence is required except on Sundays and National Holidays. The cost of a licence is only 5 esc. The Minho river contains a few salmon, but the sea trout fishing is outstanding. It is also good in the lower reaches of the Lima River. The northern rivers all contain good brown trout, as do the lakes and rivers in the highlands. Nearly all the rivers

Fishing boats

from the Tagus to the Algarve provide excellent sport with barbel and carp. The closed seasons are as follows:

Salmon. 20th October to 31st January.
Trout. 10th November to 15th February.
Coarse Fish. 1st March to 30th June.

Sea Fishing. Portugal is a sea fisherman's paradise, whether your particular passion is boat fishing or beach casting. Here are some of the best centres: In the North, Vila do Conde, Póvoa de Varzim, Ofir, Esposende and Viana do Castelo. The main sport is for bass and grey bream, with grey mullet, mackerel and pout whiting plentiful everywhere. In the central area of Portugal, Nazaré, São Martinho do Porto, Peniche, The Berlenga Islands, Ericeira, Cascais and Sesimbra are all convenient spots. Apart from bass, mullet and bream, this is the spot to go after the big fellows—swordfish, tunny, shark and tope. TAP Portuguese Airways publish an excellent little booklet for anglers giving details of fishing stations, baits, accommodation etc.

Shooting. The great majority of shooting in Portugal is free. Woodcock, snipe, partridge and hare are plentiful. At certain times of the year large numbers of migatory wild pigeon are to be taken.

A shooting licence costs 30 esc for a year.

Shooting of partridge is permitted from October 1 to January 15, but game beats are restricted to November 15 to January 1. In several resorts, such as Estoril, there are also facilities for clay pigeon shooting.

Motor Racing. Sports car meeting and Grand Prix in June at Vila Real, Lisboa or Porto. Lisboâ Grand Prix for 500 c.c. formula cars in July.

Others. All the main resorts have facilities for tennis and it is frequently possible to ride. Mini-Golf courses and, to a limited extent, Go-karting courses are also available, as is open air 10-pin bowling.

THE BULLFIGHT

Bullfighting in Portugal up to the beginning of the 18th century was fought under the same rules as Spain. That is to say, the bull was killed. However, a wealthy nobleman, the Count of Arcos was killed in the ring and the reigning king, D. José I decreed that from then on the bull's horns must be sheathed and that the *coup de grace* should be purely symbolic. Nowadays, the combat is carried out partly on foot and partly on horseback. The *cavaleiro* [kå-vå-lay'ee-roo], riding a superb horse, challenges the bull. When the bull charges, the horse side-steps and the *cavaleiro* plants a bandarilha (*ferro*) into the beast's shoulder. The passes are continued, sometimes being varied by the planting of *ferros curtos,* bandarilhas with short, broken shafts. This means that the horse and rider have to get even closer to the bull. At last, when the bull is tired and refuses to allow the *cavaleiro* to show off his passes, the chairman gives the sign for entry of the *moços de forcado*. This is the team whose job it is to capture the bull. The team leader, followed by his men, waits until the bull charges. The leader then attempts to hold the bull by putting his arms behind its horns, while the remainder of the team try to control it.

Portuguese bullfighting is neither so exciting nor so cruel as the Spanish variety. Even so, the spectacle, colour and movement make a visit well worth while. As in Spain, the seats are divided into three categories according to the amount of shade. *Sombra* (shade) are the most expensive; next come *sol e sombra,* where spectators will have the sun in their eyes part of the time; and, lastly, *sol,* where the heat will probably be too much for most visitors. These categories are themselves divided, the most expensive being the seats in the front row (*barreira*) just above the gallery between the bullring fence and the main tiered seats (*trincheira*).

Bullfighting takes place from Easter to October. The main rings are the Campo Pequeno in Lisboa. Vila Franca de Xira, Moita do Ribatejo, Alcochete, Salvaterra de Magos, Cartaxo, Vila do Conde, Figueira da Foz, Alcácer do Sal, Coruche, Santarém, Póvoa de Varzim, Moita, Golegã, Alpiarça, Almeirim and Cascais.

PORTUGUESE WEIGHTS AND MEASURES

Weight. The standard of weight is the kilogram (*quilograma*) [kee′loo grä′mä], which equals approximately 2 lb 3 oz. Other useful weights are:

100 grm = 3½ oz	5 kilos = 10 lb 12 oz
250 grm = 8¾ oz	10 kilos = 21 lb 8 oz
500 grm = 1 lb 1½ oz	30 kilos = 64 lb 8 oz

Liquid. The standard of liquid measure is the litre (*litro*) [lee′troo] which equals approximately 1¾ pints. There are about 4½ litros to the gallon.

Linear. The standard length is the metre (*metro*) [me′troo] which equals approximately 3 ft 3 ins. There are 100 *centimetros* (2/5 in) to the metre and 1000 metres to the kilometre (*quilómetros*) [kee-lo′me-troo], which is roughly 5/8 of a mile.

Clothing sizes

DRESSES AND SUITS	WOMEN						TEENAGERS					
British	36	38	40	42	44	46	32	33	35	36	38	39
American	34	36	38	40	42	44	10	12	14	16	18	20
Continental	42	44	46	48	50	52	38	40	42	44	46	48

	SHIRTS						
British and American	14	14½	15	15½	16	16½	17
Continental	36	37	38	39	41	42	43

	STOCKINGS					
British and American	8	8½	9	9½	10	10½
Continental	0	1	2	3	4	5

	SOCKS				
British and American	9½	10	10½	11	11½
Continental	38/39	39/40	40/41	41/42	42/43

	SHOES						
British and American	3	4	5	6	7	8	9	10
Continental	36	37	38	39	41	42	43	44

GLOVE sizes are the same as in Britain and America.

USEFUL ADDRESSES

Portuguese State Information and Tourist Office, Casa de Portugal, 20 Lower Regent Street, London S.W.1. *Tel:* WHItehall 2455; 570 Fifth Avenue, New York 10036. *Tel.* 581-2450.

Airlines.
B.E.A. Dorland House, Lower Regent Street, London S.W.1. *Tel*: GERrard 9833.
BOAC. Airways Terminal, Buckingham Palace Rd., London S.W.1. *Tel:* VICtoria 2323.
VARIG. 135 New Bond Street, London W.1. *Tel*: HYDe Park 4207.
Pan American World Airways, 193 Piccadilly, London W.1. *Tel:* REGent 8474; Pan Am Building, New York 10017. *Tel.* 973-4000; 30 S. Michigan, Chicago 60603. *Tel.* RA 6-6272.
TAP Portuguese Airways, 19 Lower Regent Street, London S.W.1. *Tel.* TRAfalgar 6767; 601 Fifth Avenue, New York 10017. *Tel.* 421-8500.

Shipping Lines.
Blue Star Line. 3 Lower Regent Street, London S.W.1. *Tel:* WHItehall 2266.
P & O Lines. 14 Cockspur Street, London S.W.1. *Tel:* WHItehall 4444.
Royal Mail Line. Royal Mail House, Leadenhall Street, London E.C.3. *Tel:* MANsion House 0522.
Grimaldi Siosa Line. 220 Kensington High Street, London W.8. *Tel:* WEStern 1541.
Currie Line Ltd. 107 Leadenhall Street, London E.C.3. *Tel:* AVEnue 1576.

RESORTS AND PLACES OF INTEREST

(Listed in Alphabetical Order)

ALBUFEIRA. To my mind the most attractive place in the whole of the Algarve, Albufeira is a thriving little community. It has a busy fishing harbour and is a centre of the fig and almond industries. The village street is particularly attractive with its strong Moorish atmosphere. There are several good sandy beaches actually within the boundaries of the town and there are plenty more close at hand.

A new hotel right on the front was opened in 1965 under British management. There is a bright night club and several gay little cafés and restaurants. In addition, Albufeira has one motel consisting of furnished apartments and an excellent restaurant. Although they are not cheap, I can personally recommend these *Residencias Boa Vista* as being spotlessly clean and comfortable. The restaurant serves the best food in the whole of the Algarve.

Hotels: 1 1st class, 1 estalagem, 2 pensões, 1 motel. Lisboa 312 km, Faro 38.

ALCOBAÇA (pop. 5,000), a charming town of narrow streets and open air market stalls, lies on the main road from Lisboa to Porto about 10 km inland from Nazaré and is certainly worth a visit if you are staying on the coast. The town is delightfully situated on the junction of the rivers Alcoa and Baça where, in 1154, Cistercian monks founded the Mosteiro de Santa Maria. The vast kitchens where it was possible to roast six oxen at a time have a river flowing through

Albufeira

which supplied fish—mostly eels—on Friday, and at one time the abbey was one of the richest in Portugal.

The splendid early-Gothic Church and the two-storied Cloisters are extremely beautiful, but of greatest human interest is the Capela dos Túmulos (Chapel of the two Tombs). This contains the tombs of King Pedro (1357-67) and his mistress, Inès de Castro, placed foot to foot so that at the Last Judgement they would rise to face each other. Inès was a lady-in-waiting from Galicia in northern Spain with whom Pedro fell in love while still a Prince and whom he married in secret and kept in the Quinta das Lágrimas (Villa of Tears) in Coimbra after his wife's death. This marriage was con-

Alcobaça

sidered to be politically dangerous by various courtiers who warned Pedro's father against it and, in the young prince's absence, had Inès murdered. Once he had ascended the throne, Pedro sought out the murderers and killed them with his own hands. Finally, Inès's body was brought to Alcobaça and placed in the tomb Pedro had himself designed. John, Grand Master of Aviz, was one of their illegitimate children.

Hotels: 1 2nd class, 1 pension, Estalagem do Cruzeiro *at Aljubarrota (6 km), Leiria 31 km, Lisboa 116, Santarém 65.*

ALFEIZERÃO. See SÃO MARTINHO DO PÔRTO.

ALIJÓ (pop. 5,400). This little hill town is situated in the midst of the *País do Vinho* (wine country) which is the area round the river Douro where the grapes for port are grown. The pleasant 12-roomed *Pousada do Barão de Forrester* makes it a good centre from which

to explore the Douro valley or to spend a night during a brief tour of the region.

Nearest station: Pinhão. Porto 145 km, Vila Real 49.

ALJUBARROTA, some 25 km south of Leiria, was the scene of a battle between John, Grand Master of Aviz, whom the *Cortes* declared king of Portugal in 1385 and John I of Castile. The Portuguese, aided by a small band of English archers, routed a vastly superior force of Castilians and the battle was decisive in establishing Portugal's autonomy. As a direct result of this victory the treaty of Windsor was signed in 1386, raising the Anglo-Portuguese connections to the status of a permanent alliance, and in 1387 the Portuguese king married Phillipa of Lancaster, John of Gaunt's daughter.

Aljubarrota has an excellent *estalagem* where you may well be served a delicious almond paste sweet which is made in the likeness of a baker's wife who is reputed to have slaughtered six Castilians, who had been hiding in a baking oven, with a shovel. From the *estalagem* you can comfortably visit **Batalha** (11 km) and see the magnificent Mosteiro de Santa Maria de Vitória which John caused to be built in thanks for his victory. This monastery is acknowledged to be not only the finest example of Portuguese Gothic and Manueline architecture but also one of the grandest buildings in all Europe.

Completed in the 16th century by João de Castilho, the architect of Belém, and built in golden sandstone carved into the most elaborate shapes and motifs, the Monastery (originally a Dominican convent) includes the Church with a glorious west front and the Founder's Chapel which contains the tombs

The Mosteiro de Alcobaça

Batalha: detail of cloister

of John and his wife, their children —notably that of Henry the Navigator—and other Portuguese kings. The Royal Cloister (*Claustro Real*) is a 100-foot square with richly and extravagantly carved arcades surrounding a charming garden. During the first half of the 19th century the French destroyed and pillaged various parts of the building, but these have now been largely restored and the Mosteiro is a national monument. There is fine stained glass to be seen and many other treasures; if you do no other sightseeing, try and fit in a visit to Batalha which can easily be reached from Lisboa (133 km).

AMARANTE (pop. 3,000) is a picturesque and ancient town on the banks of the Rio Tâmega, a tributary of the Douro. It is famous for its wine and on the first Saturday in June celebrates the feast of São Gonçalo who was supposed to marry off old women. Lupin seeds, which have long been associated with fertility in southern

European and Mediterranean countries, are distributed among the people and the festival has a distinct pagan flavour. In the 15th and 16th centuries Amarante was largely populated by *merranos* or Jews who, in the face of persecution, had ostensibly become Christians.

There is one 3rd class hotel but some 25 km away on the road to Vila Real is the comfortable *Pousada de São Gonçalo*.
Porto 66 km, Vila Real 49, Braga 55.

ARMAÇÃO DE PERA is an attractive little fishing village of Phoenician origin. In the centre of the sweep of the magnificent sandy bay is a casino and one excellent hotel, boasting its own night club.
*Hotels: 1 1st class, 3 pensões.
Lisboa 326 km, Tunes 25 (rail junction).*

AVEIRO (pop. 17,105). Situated on a lagoon at the mouth of the Rio Vouga, Aveiro is not a beach resort. It is, however, eminently suitable as a centre for touring this region of Portugal, and is a gay

Armação de Pera

and charming town in its own
right. There is a theatre, a hotel and
several pensões. The local tourist
office arranges boat trips on the
lagoon, the Ria d'Aveiro.

The Convent of Jesus, or Convent
of Santa Joana, named after the
daughter of Afonso V who taught
here at the end of the 15th century,
has a gilded church with fine wood
carvings and *azulejos*. The church is
15th-century, but the decorations
are 17th and 18th-century. In the
Regional Museum, which is housed
in an annexe of the church, is a
portrait of Santa Joana, probably
by Nuno Gonçalves. Next to the
convent stands the Cathedral of
Nossa Senhora da Gloria, a 16th-
century building with an 18th-
century granite façade. In front of
the Cathedral is a particularly fine
16th-century calvary.

*Hotels: 1 2nd class, 3 pensões.
Trains: Northern line. Buses to
Anadia, Agueda, Curia, Mealhada
and Coimbra; Ilhavo, Mira, Tocha,
and Figueira da Foz; Albergaria a
Velha, Oliveira de Azeméis, and
Vale de Cambra. Porto 70 km,
Figueira da Foz 63, Viana do
Castelo 142.*

AZEITÃO. A small village a little
way inland from Portinho da
Arrábida, some seven miles from
the sea. It is the centre of an
important wine producing area
and would make an excellent centre
for a touring holiday in the region.

The Quinta de Bacalhoa, a fine
old estate with a magnificent house,
has recently been restored, and the
owner will allow visitors to look
around on application to the lodge.

The *Estalagem Quinta das Torres*
is an ancient estate house, part of
which is still lived in by the original
family. There are now several
suites and half a dozen rooms in the
hotel side, all furnished with period
pieces in exquisite taste. There is a

Calvary at Aveiro

lake for swimming and acres of
beautiful grounds. In summer one
dines outside and light is provided
throughout the hotel by candles.
Lisboa 27 km, Setúbal 13.

BARCELOS (pop. 5,000). Situated
on the Rio Cávado, Barcelos is
a centre of the pottery industry,
pink cocks and flower-dotted hens
being fired in dome-shaped, char-
coal-fired kilns by the roadside.
Barcelos was the seat of the first
earldom in Portugal which subsequently became the House of
Braganza. The main square, the
Campo da Feira, is one of the most
beautiful in Portugal, being nearly a
quarter of a mile across and having
an ornamental fountain in the
middle. One side of the square is
occupied by the Capuchin convent
built in 1649 and now a hospital.
On the west side in the corner is the
flamboyant octagonal Church of
Senhor da Cruz. This church is
extremely beautiful inside and
nobody visiting the town should
miss the richly carved side altars.
On the north of the square is

another church of interest, the Oblates' Church of St Benedict. There are many panels on the ceiling illustrating the works of the saint. *Hotel: 1 2nd class pensão. Trains: Minho and Braga line. Buses to Porto, Braga, Esposende, Póvoa de Varzim. Porto 50 km, Braga 17, Viana do Castelo 30.*

BARREIRO. Across the Rio Tejo (Tagus) from Lisboa, this little town is reached by ferry. The boats connect with trains to southern Portugal at Barreiro terminus. If you have to wait for your train, it is worth taking a bus or taxi to Montijo, near which is a chapel dedicated to Our Lady of Atalaia. This is the object of many pilgrimages and the scene of a *romaria* [roo-må-ree'å] (religious festival) during the last week-end in August.

BATALHA. See ALJUBARROTA.

BEJA (pop. 16,000). A large agricultural centre, Beja is princi-

pally known now for the convent of Nossa Senhora da Conceição from which the Portuguese nun Marianna Alcoforado is reputed to have written her famous letters to a French officer. I think that the convent is rather ugly but there are some fine details such as the doorway of the chapter house. The town has an archaeological museum and the old hospital (late 15th-century) is worth a visit. The Castle, once a formidable building with forty towers, is mostly 18th-century, but the 14th-century keep is interesting, having been built by D. Diniz (1279-1325).
Hotels: 1 3rd class, 4 pensões (2 1st class, 2 2nd class). Lisboa 185 km, Vila Real de Santo António 143, Sines 95, Vidigueira 25.

THE BERLENGA ISLANDS. An hour's journey by launch from Peniche. The launch leaves every morning during the season June to September (two journeys on

Amarante on the banks of the Rio Tamega

Beja

Sundays) and returns in the evening.

The Berlengas offer magnificent fishing, swimming and skin-diving, but there is nothing else to do. Marvellous for an away-from-it-all holiday. The *Pousada de São João Baptista* is an old converted fortress.

Hotel: 1 pousada, residence limited to five days. Lisboa 95 km.

BRAGA (pop. 32,600). In Roman times, Braga was an important centre and was occupied in turn by the Suevi, the Goths, and the Moors. It was finally restored to Christian rule in A.D. 1040 by Ferdinand of Castile. Roman Catholics will be interested in the fact that Braga, under an edict of the Council of Trent has retained its own liturgy and rites.

From a tangled web of old streets a mass of towers and belfries rises from the many churches. The Cathedral or Sé was built in Romanesque style at the end of the 11th century. Since then there have been so many additions, alterations and restorations that it is difficult at times to sort out one from the other. Nevertheless there are some lovely individual details such as the Madonna over the north altar and the Romanesque south door.

There are so many churches in Braga worth seeing—the tiny chapel of Nossa Senhora da Torre in the pretty little Largo de S. Paulo square, the octagonal Chapel of S. Sebastião, the highly ornamental Church of S. Vicente and the great pilgrimage Church of Bom Jesus standing on a hill outside the town.

Three other buildings that should be seen by the visitor are: the Church of S. Frutuoso, almost certainly built before the Moors came to Portugal and probably restored in the 11th century; the Monastery of Tibâes (only the church is now in use, the remainder of the huge building belonging to a private family); and finally, the Chapel of S. Maria Madalena in the

Braga

Serra da Falperra, 4 km south of Braga.
Hotels: 2 3rd class, 7 pensões. Trains: Minho and Braga line. Buses to nearby towns including Porto, Póvoa de Varzim, Viana do Castelo and Esposende. Porto 50 km, Barcelos 17, Viana do Castelo 47, Guimarães 22.

BRAGANÇA (pop. 8,250). Standing two thousand feet above sea level, the city is dominated by the medieval fortress with its old walls and a tower nearly 100 ft high. The buildings are still used as army barracks and the great square is now the parade ground.

There are many beautiful buildings in Bragança including several churches of note, the Church of S. João Baptista being outstanding. The Largo de Sepúlveda, one of the main squares, has some lovely buildings including the Church of S. Vicente where D. Pedro the Cruel is said to have married Inès de Castro. In more recent times, Bragança was the scene of the revolution against the French general Junot during the Peninsular War.
Hotels: 1 pousada, 2 pensões. Porto 253 km, Chaves 91, Vila Real 138, Vinhais 33.

BUÇACO. See COIMBRA.

CACILHAS is the nearest point to Lisboa across the Rio Tejo and is reached by ferry. The town itself is of little interest and not in any sense a resort. However, it is a good starting point from which to explore the *Outra Banda* and is a major terminal for buses to the Serra da Arrábida and the whole of the south of Portugal. Its other claim to fame is the number of excellent sea food restaurants to be found in the town. A pleasant evening can be had by walking past the huge

modern monument to Christ the King, at Almada, before dining at one of the restaurants overlooking the river with the twinkling lights of Lisboa beyond.
Setúbal 39 km.

CARCAVELOS. About half-way between Lisboa and Estoril, this little resort makes a useful centre. You can choose between the beaches to the east or the bright lights to the west. Communications are good and accommodation cheaper than in Estoril or Lisboa.
Hotels: 1 2nd class, 1 estalagem, 1 pensao. Trains: Lisboa to Cascais suburban line. Lisboa 21 km.

CASCAIS (pop. 7,950). Known the world over as the retreat of deposed monarchs, Cascais has up to now been primarily a fishing port, hampered in its effort to become a resort by lack of hotel accommodation. It has a magnificent beach, good restaurants, and first rate connections to Lisboa by fast electric suburban trains. The con-

Cascais

struction of a new 1st class hotel will ensure its popularity in the future.

The Church of Nossa Senhora da Assunção is in Manueline style and has 18th-century tiles. There are some interesting 16th and 17th-century paintings in the Santissimo Chapel and the crypt. Two other churches are worthy of a visit. First, the Misericórdia, containing a portrait of Nossa Senhora dos Anjos. It was built in 1751 and never finished. The other is the Church of the Navigators, octagonal in shape and devoted to seafarers.

The Castro Guimaraes Museum is housed in a fine old villa and contains some 19th-century paintings, some rare pieces of faïence, a magnificent library and a section devoted to archaeology.

Cascais has sailing regattas, horse shows, and car rallies of international standard. There is one of the finest bullrings in the country and a large stadium is being constructed to provide facilities for football, hockey, roller skating etc. It will also include a theatre. There are facilities for golf and tennis nearby.

Hotels: 2 1st class, 3 estalagens, 3 pensões. There is a large new hotel between Cascais and Estoril. Trains: fast suburban service to Estoril and Lisboa. Buses to Colares and Sintra, Alcabideche and Estoril. Lisboa 28 km, Sintra 25, Ericeira 47, Vila Franca de Xira 59.

CASTELO BRANCO. A bustling town, and a useful stopping place if driving from Madrid to Lisboa. From an architectural point of view there is little of outstanding interest but if it is term-time try to see the Lyceum in what was once the Bishop's Palace. This is set in a great formal garden of terraces with an imposing staircase dotted with statues. The municipal offices are now housed in an old 17th-century palace which is worth a quick look, as it is next to the regional museum. There are some old Flemish tapestries and some interesting, but badly restored, paintings.

Hotels: 1 1st class, 2 pensões. Lisboa 264 km, frontier at Piedras Albas 60, Abrantes 195, Lardosa 19.

CAVALOS DO FÃO. A little village on the left bank of the Rio Cávado near Ofir. There are attractive pine woods between the main road and the sea.

Hotel: 1 1st class estalagem. Porto 46 km, Viana do Castelo 14.

COIMBRA (pop. 45,000). This fine old university town on the banks of the Rio Mondego was at one time the capital of Portugal. Six kings were born here and, from the middle of the 11th century, it was the centre of the drive against the Moors. The University is the oldest and, until 1911, was the only university in Portugal. Founded in 1290 in Lisboa, it was transferred to Coimbra in 1307 in compensation for the court's removal to the present Portuguese capital, but it was finally established only in 1537. It occupies a magnificent position 300 ft above the river and the chairs of modern languages, mathematics, physics and medicine were founded in 1772 when the formidable Portuguese statesman, Pombal, re-organised the university. He also designed the observatory and laid out the botanical gardens which contain many sub-tropical plants. Although many of the original buildings have been altered and modernised at the instigation of Doctor Salazar, the beautiful library (1728) consisting of three enormous rooms with attractive galleries and painted ceilings still remains. Of the three million volumes and

Coimbra: Santa Maria do Celas

3,000 manuscripts the first edition
of Camões's *Os Lusíadas* is the most
interesting for the layman and is
usually on exhibition with other
rarities.

In the centre of the town is the
monastery of Santa Cruz which is
basically a 12th-century building
with later additions—notably a
charming Renaissance sacristy
which contains several fine pictures
of the Portuguese school. The
western façade of the church is
magnificently carved and the 16th-
century pulpit of Jean de Rouen is
quite exquisite. The walls of the
church are covered with *azulejos*
and the upper choir, reached by a
stair from the two-storied cloisters,
contains unique choir-stalls, the
backs depicting the voyages of
Vasco da Gama.

If you have time you should visit
the Museum (Museu Machado de
Castro) which is in the Bishop's
Palace in the Largo de Feira.
Apart from Roman finds, Romanesque and Gothic sculptures and
furniture and faïence, there are
several important Flemish paintings

and modern Portuguese works.
Across the river are the remains of
the old Convent of Santa Clara
which was destroyed by floods—
you now enter it by boat—and
beside it is the villa where Inès de
Castro was murdered (see ALCO-
BAÇA). The new convent was built
during the second half of the 17th
century and contains the shrine and
tomb of Queen Isabella, wife of
King Diniz (1279-1325) and patron
saint of the city.

Some 30 km north east of
Coimbra are the incredibly beautiful **Woods of Buçaco** near Luso.
Here you walk amidst gigantic
cedars from Lebanon and the
Himalayas, trees native to Portugal
and many exotic trees which were
brought back from the Americas by
Portuguese explorers in the 16th
century. It was at Buçaco that
Wellington finally defeated Marshall
Masséna and drove the French out
of Portugal (1810). There is a small
military museum in the Carmelite
Monastery by the 'neo-manueline'
Palace Hotel—a late 19th-century
hunting lodge built by King Carlos.
*Hotels: 2 1st class (the Astoria is
good), 4 3rd class, 1 estalagem (of
which I have good reports), 8
pensões. Lisboa 204 km, Porto 117,
Figueira da Foz 45, Aveiro 55.*

COLARES. See PRAIA DAS MAÇÃS.

COVILHA. See FUNDÃO.

DONA ANA. A tiny cove backed
by towering cliffs and with a small
tree-studded island in the mouth of
the bay. There are masses of little
sandy bays to explore and the caves
and grottos at Ponto da Piedade
are close by.
*Hotel: 1 pensão, the Dona Ana,
which is clean and comfortable. The
owners speak English. A hotel car
can meet guests at Lagos station
by arrangement. Lisboa 268 km,
Lagos 1½.*

Maize vat in North Portugal

ELVAS (pop. 12,000), situated in the plain of Alentejo, is a small manufacturing and market town, producing jewellery and firearms and providing a market for locally-produced olive oil, plums, wine and grain. It is an old fortified frontier town just 18 km from Badajoz across the Spanish border and was originally fortified by the Moors. They were driven out in 1226, but it still retains a Moorish flavour and the graceful aqueduct of Amoreira is a magnificent example of their engineering abilities. There are several rich churches of which the 16th-century octagonal Church of São Domingo is covered from floor to ceiling with *azulejos*. The *Pousada de Santa Luzia* is just outside the walls, has a good cuisine and an atmosphere redolent of Alentejo.
Hotels: 1 2nd class, 1 pousada. Estremoz 42 km, Portalegre 52, Lisboa 205.

ERICEIRA (pop. 2,530). A charming little fishing port, market town and seaside resort, within easy reach, by car, of Lisboa. The village is situated on cliffs, and has a small sandy beach. It is known for lobster breeding, and the thermal baths of Santa Maria. It is from Ericeira that the Portuguese Royal Family sailed into exile in 1910.

The *Hotel de Turismo* (1st class) is beautifully situated on the cliffs overlooking the bay, and has its own night club, swimming pools for adults and children, and a terrace for drinks. It also has tanks of lobsters on the beach from which you can choose your own meal. The *Estalagem Pedro O Pescador* is also excellent but early booking is essential.
Hotels: 1 1st class, 2 estalagens, 4 pensões. Buses to Lisboa (via Mafra), Sintra. Lisboa 51 km, Sintra 22, Torres Vedras 47.

ESPINHO (pop. 8,037). A small industrial town, principally concerned with fish canning. It is also a popular seaside resort with a good beach, a casino, swimming pool, golf course, bullfights and a theatre.
Hotels: 1 2nd class, 1 3rd class, 1 pensao. Trains: Northern line. Buses to Porto and Lourosa. Porto 19 km, Angeja 40, Viseu 127, Coimbra 105.

ESPOSENDE is a little town on the right bank of the Rio Cávado and is an ideal spot for a quiet holiday. There is a fine sweep of sandy beach and good fishing in the estuary. There are a few pleasant small cafés and a 2nd class hotel, the *Suave Mar*, only a stone's throw from the beach. It has a private swimming pool and there is dancing to records in the evenings. *Porto 48 km.*

ESTORIL and **MONTE ESTORIL** are twin towns on Portugal's Costa do Sol and together make

Estoril

up Portugal's largest and most fashionable resort, the playground of Europe's deposed monarchs and international sportsmen. The town is linked to Lisboa by an excellent transportation system. The beach is of fine sand and there are two municipal swimming pools for use when the tide goes out as the lower part of the beach is covered in rocks. The casino has a theatre, restaurant, night club, concert hall and, of course, gaming rooms and is beautifully situated on a hill covered with refreshing gardens. There is a superb 18-hole golf course where temporary membership can be arranged. Green fees are 66 esc (16s. 6d. or $2.25) on weekdays and 105 esc (£1 6s. 3d. or $3.60) on Saturdays, Sundays and holidays. A ticket for 15 days costs 500 esc (£6 5s. or $17.25). In addition there are two tennis clubs, a mini-golf course, facilities for pigeon shooting and riding, every kind of water sport, and concerts and art exhibitions are constantly being arranged.

There are coach tours to Arrábida, Sesimbra, Lisboa and the Palace of Queluz and Nazaré throughout the season as well as to other places of interest. A fortnight in Estoril passes all too quickly and any spare time you have can be spent in going from restaurant to restaurant, each of which specialises in a national dish. Try the crayfish at the *Faroleiro* or delicious sole at the *Tamariz*. In the Arcadas do Parque there are several fashionable shops. Estoril has accommodation to suit every taste including the *Hotel das Arcadas* which contains 43 service flats, three good *estalagens* with plenty of character (about 144 esc per day for full board) and six first class *pensões* which are simpler, but are clean and have good food (80 esc per day). In all cases early reservations are essential.

Hotels: 1 de luxe, 4 1st class, 3 estalagens, 7 pensões. Trains: Electric line to Lisboa and Cascais (frequent services). Buses to Sintra, Alcabideche, Cascais. Lisboa 26 km.

ESTREMOZ (pop. 10,000). The town stands on a flat plain dominated by a hill on which towers the castle. It was in this castle, built in 1281 by D. Diniz, that his wife St Elizabeth of Portugal died. Later the room in which she died was made into a chapel with scenes of her life painted on the walls. It is not easy to get into the castle as it is often closed but it is worth making the effort as the view from the top of the keep is magnificent.

The Town Hall occupies a beautiful old convent building and the nearby Misericórdia Church and Hospital were once a convent of the Knights of Malta. Another historic building worth a visit, but also difficult to get into, is the former Convent of S. Francisco which is now a military barracks.

Many of the houses in Estremoz have few if any windows. This is because the climate in this part of Portugal is particularly extreme. The lack of windows keeps the houses cool in the blazing heat of summer and warm in winter. The weather, too, is probably why the women of the Alentejo, as the region is called, wear felt hats rather like a man's homburg.

Hotels: 1 3rd class, 1 pensão. Lisboa 182 km, Évora 72, Badajoz (Spain) 60, Portalegre 55.

ÉVORA (pop. 40,000). Once a centre of Celto-Iberian culture, Évora was rebuilt by the Romans, conquered by the Goths and re-captured by the Portuguese in the 12th century. Between the 12th and 16th centuries it was one of the favourite seats of the court, and consequently there are a vast number of old palaces and churches of this and earlier periods. The town is still surrounded by its medieval walls and everywhere you turn you see beautiful little squares,

Évora

lofty arches and the spires and domes of countless churches. Outside the city walls there is the odd battlemented church of S. Brás. In the same street, but inside the walls, is the church of S. Francisco which has an interesting charnel house, Gothic tombs and some Primitive paintings. Between the church of S. Francisco and the Misericórdia is the ruined church of Graça. This should be seen for the fine double cloister and the impressive classical façade. The Cathedral was consecrated in the early part of the 13th century but there have been many additions since. Architecturally it is interesting, but although individual details are lovely, the whole could not be called beautiful. In the centre of the town in the Praça do Geraldo is an attractive 16th-century fountain, while on the north side there is the Church of S. Antão built in 1557.

Évora library contains nearly 60,000 books, many of which are extremely old. There is also a unique collection of old manuscripts. Behind the library is the monastery of the Lóios built in the late 15th century. There are some 18th-century *azulejos* and a finely proportioned cloister and chapter house.

The Largo de Alexandre Herculano has some fine old palaces and in the Largo de Joaquim António de Aguiar is the 16th-century church of Calvario which has a lovely two-storied cloister.

Archaeologists may be interested in the large number of neolithic remains that are to be found in the vicinity, and those interested in painting will enjoy joining the speculation as to who painted the great retable of *The Virgin in Glory Crowned by Angels,* originally forming the high altar of the Cathedral and now hanging in the museum.

Every visitor should visit the excellent, typical Portuguese restaurant, the *Gião.* The food is outstanding and prices are very reasonable. There is not much accommodation in the town but the *Pensão O Eborense* is outstanding.

Faro

The *Pousada dos Lóios* has just been opened in the old convent.
Hotels: 4 pensões. Trains to Lisboa by the Southern and Évora line. Buses to Setúbal and the surrounding towns. Lisboa 156 km, Portel 41, Estremoz 72, Elvas 88.

FARO is one of the largest towns in the Algarve, and with the building of the new airport will grow still larger. Near the town there are extensive sand dunes and large salt water lagoons. There is a Renaissance cathedral with a fine wooden roof and a relic chapel with baroque gilt reliquaries. If you should happen to be in the area on the 16th July, there is a large fair which takes place outside the Carmo church which was built in the early 18th century.
Hotels: 2 new 1st class, 1 3rd class, 4 pensões. Lisboa 300 km, Olhão 10, Tavira 30, Vila Real de Santo António 53, São Braz de Alportel 17, Lagos 80.

Evora: Church of S. Brás

FÁTIMA. In 1917 three 'young shepherd girls were visited by the Blessed Virgin. Our Lady appeared to the girls on the 13th of every month from May till October. Now the faithful visit Fátima on these days to make a pilgrimage to the sanctuary erected on the spot. The ceremonies consist of a torchlight procession, open air mass and the passing of the Blessed Sacrament among the sick and ailing. Needless to say, accommodation is at a premium around the 13th of the month between May and October. If at all possible, visitors should try and book well ahead for either the *Hotel de Fátima* or the guest house run by the Dominican order.

Hotels: 1 hotel, 1 estalagem, 9 pensões. Lisboa 142 km, Nazaré 60.

FERREIRA DO ALENTEJO (pop. 9,000) lies on the main road from Sevilla to Lisboa and has a pleasant *pensao* as well as the comfortable *Estalagem Eva*. It is thus a useful staging point if you are driving up from Cádiz or Gibraltar, or if you are driving south to the Algarve, it is only some 100 miles from the main resorts. The church is 16th-century.

Hotels: 1 pensão, 1 estalagem. Albufeira 165 km, Lagos 153, Faro 141, Lisboa 155.

FIGUEIRA DA FOZ (pop. 10,400). One of the oldest and best known holiday resorts in Portugal, yet sufficiently remote from Lisboa and Porto to remain uncrowded. Figueira da Foz has a magnificent two-mile stretch of golden sands, protected by the high ground of the Serra da Boa Viagem. Coimbra is only 32 km away and makes a good day excursion by bus or car. By way of amusements, the town has a swimming pool, a licensed casino, a bullring and tennis courts.

Figueira da Foz

The town is on the mouth of the Rio Mondego and is composed of two parts: the so-called 'old quarter' dating back to the 19th century, and the new quarter, which has wide, straight streets containing most of the hotels. Three km west of Figueira is the little fishing village of **Buarcos** with colourful cottages and fishing boats on the beach. There are also two 16th-century pillories in the village.

The Museum has a collection of archaeological remains and a room devoted to contemporary art. The Misericórdia in the Santo António Monastery was rebuilt in 1725.

Hotels: 1 1st class, 2 2nd class, 3 3rd class, 1 estalagem, 8 pensões. Trains: terminus of Western line. Buses to Mira, Ilhavo and Aveiro; Buarcos, Montemor O Velho and Coimbra; Monte Real and Leiria. Lisboa 204 km, Porto 130, Coimbra 45, Aveiro 63.

FOZ DO ARELHO. A small resort with a magnificent beach near the tidal lagoon of Óbidos, which provides good fishing, sailing and shooting. The nearest railway station is Caldas da Rainha and there are taxi connections. This is not a spot for night life, but ideal

for a quiet beach and sporting holiday.
Hotels: 1 2nd class, 1 pensão. Lisboa 100 km.

FUNDÃO (pop. 4,000) is an attractive village in the Cova de Beira, the valley of the Rio Zêzere. It is surrounded by orchards which form a delightful contrast to the bleak Serra Guardunha and Serra da Estrêla (ski-ing at **Penhas da Saúde)** and is 20 km from **Covilhã** which has an important textile industry. In Fundão stay at the *Estalagem da Neve* (the 'Inn of Snow').
Hotels: 1 estalagem. Castelo Branco 42 km, Guarda 66.

GUARDA (pop. 10,000). A picturesque town of character standing 3,600 ft up on the edge of the Serra da Estrêla. It is the highest town in Portugal and is a popular health resort. Although it is an ancient town and has many attractive arcades, apart from the Cathedral and the baroque façade of the Misericórdia Church, there is little of real historical or artistic interest.

The Cathedral is 15th-century and a copy of the one in Batalha.
Hotels: 1 1st class, 3 pensões. Lisboa 372 km, Porto 224, Viseu 86, Spanish frontier 50, Covilha 46, Coimbra 167.

GUIMARÃES. Once capital of Portugal, Guimarães is now a pretty little country town and centre of the linen industry. Tourists will be interested in the archaeological museum, the Museu Sarmento, which contains many prehistoric remains. There is also a collection of polychrome sculpture in a smaller museum in the cloister and annex of the Church of Nossa Senhora da Oliveira.

Towering over the city is the 12th-

Guimarães: 12th century castle

century castle, below it the palace of the Dukes of **Braganza**. Halfway between the two is the small Church of S. Miguel do Castelo where D. Afonso Henriques was baptised. This church, being so to speak a 'chapel royal', still comes directly under Rome and does not belong to the diocese. There is one hotel, but you are best advised to stay at the *Estalagem de São Pedro* in nearby Riba de Ave.
Porto 62 km, Braga 22, Vila Real 82, Viana do Castelo 69, Chaves 143.

GUINCHO has one of the finest beaches in Portugal, fringed with pines and with the Serra of Sintra in the background. Comparatively wild at the moment, it is scheduled for tourist development. For the time being, there is no bus service to Lisboa, Estoril or Cascais, so a car would be an advantage. There is a de luxe hotel, the *Hotel do Guincho,* which is a converted ancient fort. This is really luxurious and beautifully furnished with period furniture.
Hotels: 1 de luxe, 2 estalagens. Lisboa 40 km, Cascais 10.

ÍLHAVO (pop. 12,480). A fishermen's town on the Ria de Vagos. The municipal museum has a section devoted to the history of fishing and the sea, which includes paintings and miniatures of ships, amongst these being an 18th-century war galley of ivory. Another section is devoted to local porcelain and crystal.

There is no accommodation of tourist standard.

Buses to Figueira da Foz and Aveiro. Porto 74 km, Aveiro 7, Figueira da Foz 56, Viseu 105.

LAGOS. The terminus for the railway line from Tunes, Lagos is a gay little town with plenty of small cafés and restaurants. There is a dance hall and facilities for tennis. To the west there are the caves and cliffs of Ponta da Piedade and to the east a 15-mile stretch of sandy beach.

The *Hotel da Meia Praia* (1st class) has a private sandy beach, tennis courts and a lovely garden. The train from Tunes to Lagos will stop by request at the hotel's own halt. Alternatively you can take a taxi from Lagos or ask the hotel car to meet you.

Hotels: 1 1st class, 1 estalagem, 3 pensões, some bungalow apartments, the Residencias Marsol. Lisboa 269 km, Faro 80, Tavira 110, Sagres 33, Sao Braz de Alportel 82.

LAMÉGO (pop. 7,500). This lovely old town is unique in that practically every building is Baroque. Wherever you look there are beautiful old houses, churches and palaces. The bishop's palace is now a museum containing many of the contents of the Chagas convent, now demolished. There are also some good polychrome statues including two 14th-century figures of Our Lady and a collection of fine old tapestries. The Cathedral itself has been so altered and restored that it is of little interest, but it has some pleasant chapels and a very beautiful Renaissance cloister. Outside the town is the pilgrimage church of Nossa Senhora dos Remedios. A great fair is held here between the 1st and 15th of September each year. The Church itself is not particularly interesting, but the approach up an enormous double staircase is impressive.

Hotels: 1 1st class estalagem. Porto 155 km, Vila Real 40, Viseu 70, Bragança 78.

LEIRIA (pop. 8,500). A useful halfway house when driving between Lisboa and Porto. The old castle of D. Diniz stands on a rock in the middle of Rio Liz. It has been almost entirely rebuilt. There is a museum in what was once the bishop's palace.

Hotels: 1 3rd class (of which I hear good reports), 1 estalagem, 5 pensões. Lisboa 151 km, Porto 188.

LISBOA (LISBON) (pop. 817,350). Founded by the early Phoenician traders, Lisboa, like Rome, was originally built on seven hills. A disastrous earthquake in 1755 practically destroyed the city and very little of the old part remains. After the earthquake, the Marquis of Pombal rebuilt the city centre in a series of squares and avenues bordered on one side by the Rio Tejo (Tagus). The river is really Lisboa's heart. Ocean liners tie up within a few hundred yards of the main squares. Ferry boats carrying workers, tourists and their cars are constantly embarking and disembarking their passengers. Fishing craft with colourful sails and barges with loads of agricultural produce come and go, giving an air of bustle and movement.

Lisboa can be divided, roughly speaking, into three main sections.

Leiria seen from the Sanctuary of Our Lady of the Incarnation

Lisboa: Praça do Comércio

First, the main shopping and business centre clustered around the Rossio, officially called the Praça de Dom Pedro IV, and the Praça do Comércio, better known to tourists as Black Horse Square. Then there are the ancient sections of the city, consisting of the Moorish quarter to the west, and the Alfama, dominated by the Castelo de São Jorge (St George's Castle) to the east. Finally, there is the new Lisboa with modern hotels and blocks of flats stretching away towards the airport. During the daytime the central district (The Baixa) is always crowded, but at 7.30 or so, when commercial life ceases, activity is transferred to the Rossio, the Praça dos Restauradores and the cafés which line the pavements of the Avenida da

69

Liberdade. In summertime these cafés are gay with striped umbrellas by day, and a glittering fairyland of coloured lights by night. Another popular spot for the Portuguese in the evenings is the gigantic fairground on the outskirts of the city at Palhavã Park.

Lisboa is not merely a beautiful capital city with ancient buildings and fine hotels. It is a wonderful holiday centre with literally dozens of beaches on your doorstep and a bewildering variety of possible excursions. Probably no other capital city has so much to offer the holidaymaker, and costs, though rising slowly, are still low by our standards.

Mosteiro Dos Jerónimos (Jeronimos Monastery) at Belém is the largest monument in Lisboa. It is often said to have been erected to commemorate Vasco da Gama's voyage to the Indies. This is not so. The building was started before the voyage took place. It was commissioned by King Manoel I on the site of a chapel founded by the Infante Henrique the Navigator. The general design is the work of Boytaca, but he was succeeded by João de Castilho and his young assistant, Nicolas Chanterne. It was Chanterne, a sculptor, who was to introduce Renaissance art to Portugal. Jerónimos Monastery is probably the finest example of Manueline architecture in the country. It is decorated with the ropes, shells, anchors and strange plants so typical of the school and the age which it represents. The church itself contains many royal tombs, and in one of the confessional boxes lies the body of President Sidónio Pais, who was assassinated in 1918. The cloister, with its two superimposed and richly carved white limestone arches is quite lovely. Off it can be found the

Lisboa: Jerónimos cloister

refectory, the chapter house containing the tomb of President Carmona, and the upper choir of the church which has a wooden figure of Christ dating back to the 16th century.

The Tower of Belém was built in the early part of the 16th century by Francisco of Arruda to the order of King Manoel. Originally in the middle of the river, the encroaching sands have now surrounded it and the tower stands on a small promontory. It is essentially a Manueline building with strong overtones of Moorish, especially in the roof and domes over the towers and loggia. There are wonderful views over the river from the 2nd and 3rd floors.

The Monument to the Discoverers, Praça de Boa Esperança, Belém, was inaugurated in 1960. This vast monument commemorates the great voyages of discovery undertaken by Prince Henry the Navigator's

Monument to the Discoverers

sailors. It is, in spite of its bulk and solidity, extremely graceful and impressive.

Sé Patriarchal (Lisboa Cathedral), Largo da Sé. The original building was erected in the 12th century. Rebuilt in 1755, it was badly damaged by the earthquake and subsequent restorations have left the remains of the Romanesque building, part of the façade and the general design. The cloister, although badly damaged, is 13th-century. The Cathedral is open from 9 a.m. to 5 p.m. and a charge is made for a guided tour. The Cathedral possesses a remarkable collection of treasures, including the Philippine Cross, but these are very rarely on public show.

Ruinas do Convento do Carmo (The Carmo Church), Largo do Carmo. Begun in 1389, the convent was destroyed by the earthquake

of 1755. The church is now the archaelogical museum, but the ruins are interesting in their own right, particularly the former nave, now open to the sky and lawned.

Basílica da Estrêla (The Estrela Church), Praça da Estrêla. Built between 1779 and 1790 by Matheus Vicente and Reinaldo Manuel to fulfil a vow made by Queen Maria I. The church is, to my mind, too highly decorated in a fussy style to be beautiful. There is, however, a wonderful view from the cupola.

Igreja da Madre de Deus (Mother of God Church), 4 Rua da Madre de Deus. Formerly belonging to a convent, the church was founded in 1509 by Dona Leonor, widow of João II. There is a Manueline door bearing Dona Leonor's crest (the net) and her husband's (the pelican). In the choir and sacristy there are some 16th-century paintings and in the sub-choir and cloister some good 16th-century glazed tiles.

Igreja de São Roque (St Roque Church), Largo Trinidade Coelho. Built by F. Terzi at the end of the 16th century, the building was damaged during the great earthquake of 1755 and the façade, which collapsed, was rebuilt. The interior is decorated with mosaics, wood carvings and glazed tiles. The ceiling is particularly fine, being ornamented with 16th-century paintings on wood. The fifth chapel on the left hand side, dedicated to São João Baptista, was built in 1742 by King João V. It is richly decorated with marbles and mosaics, ivory and lapis-lazuli.

Igreja de São Vicente de Fora (St Vincent Church), Largo de São Vicente. This beautiful church was rebuilt from 1582 to 1627 by

Filippo Terzi. It is one of the loveliest buildings of the Renaissance period. The monks' refectory is now the resting place of all the kings and queens of the House of Braganza.

Castelo de São Jorge (St George's Castle), which has looked down on the city since Roman times, is a fund of history and architectural interest. Some of the walls and towers date back to the time of the Visigoths. In the north part of the walls is the Martim Moniz Gate where a Portuguese horseman sacrificed his life by placing himself and his horse across the entrance, enabling the Portuguese troops to enter and destroy the Moorish defenders. Up to the time of D. Manuel, the castle was the royal residence. The view of the city is particularly fine when the sun is setting over the city and the river.

All **Museums** in Lisboa are closed on Mondays. Admission from Tuesday to Sunday inclusive usually costs about 2 esc 50 (7½d.). The best time is between 11 a.m. and 5 p.m.

Lisboa: old quarter

Museu Nacional de Arte Antiga, 95 Rua das Janelas Verdes. One of Europe's finest museums. Contains a collection of paintings, silver, pottery, jewelry and tapestry. In room 11 is the famous work by Nuno Gonçalves depicting Henry the Navigator surrounded by all the famous figures of Portugal's Golden Age. There is not space in a book of this sort to deal with all the works of art housed in this museum. Suffice it to say that anyone interested in Portugal's history, art and silverware should be prepared to spend at least half a day in this museum.

Museu Arqueologico de Carmo, Largo do Carmo, contains prehistoric and mediaeval relics, sarcophagi, sculpture, pottery etc., and is housed in the ruins of the Carmo church.

There are many other museums in Lisboa. For example Museu Militar, Largo do Museu de Artilharia, where there is a large collection of armour, weapons, uniforms etc. dating from the 15th century up to the present time. Museu da Cidade, Palácio da Mitra, 64 Rua do Açúcar, contains engravings, tiles, drawings and documents relating to the history of the capital, housed in an ancient palace. Museu Nacional de Arte Contemporânea, 6 Rua Serpa Pinto, contains the works of modern Portuguese artists. Museu de Arte Decorativa, Largo das Portas do Sol, Alfama, is an old palace decorated with works of art made in Portugal during the 17th and 18th centuries. The adjoining schools of book-binding and gold-beating can also be visited. Museu Nacional dos Coches, Praça Afonso de Albuquerque, Belém, contains a unique and fascinating collection of royal and state coaches, harness etc. housed in the former royal riding school.

Drying clothes in Lisboa

Aquário Vasco da Gama (Aquarium) Avenida Marginal, Dafundo, contains various fish found off the coasts of Portugal and the overseas provinces. There is also the Oceanographic Collection which belonged to King Carlos I.

There are many gardens and parks in Lisboa where you can relax after sightseeing. The Campo Grande Gardens have pleasant, cool walks, boating in the lake, a restaurant and café. Parque Eduardo VII, at the top of Avenida da Liberdade, is a beautiful park with a wonderful show of flowers and a breath-taking view down the whole length of the Avenida da Liberdade. See the *Estufa Fria,* a huge cold greenhouse with a riot of tropical vegetation, waterfalls and fish pools. It is very cool in hot weather. Parque Florestal de Monsanto (Monsanto Park), Monsanto, is a very large expanse of wooded park land on the outskirts of Lisboa. Jardim Zoologico (Zoological Gardens), 158 Estrada de Benfica, Laranjeiras, is one of the

finest zoos in Europe, with a large collection of wild animals and beautiful rose gardens.

There are fine viewpoints scattered around the seven hills of Lisboa, usually consisting of a car park, gardens and sometimes small cafés. Three of them are: *Montes Claros, Parque Florestal de Monsanto; S. Pedro de Alcantara, Rua S. Pedro de Alcantara; Santa Luzia, Largo das Portas do Sol.*

Restaurants. There are hundreds of restaurants in Lisboa, and one of the delights of foreign travel is to shop around for one's meal by inspecting the menus outside. However, I will give here just four restaurants where you can eat the best of Portuguese food:
Restaurante Polícia, Rua Marques Sá da Bandeira. This is a short taxi ride from the centre of the city and is my personal favourite. You go in through the wine cellar and through the kitchen. The food is very good, as is the wine. The surroundings are simple and friendly. You can't spend much

Street café in Lisboa

money here, however hard you try. *Restaurante Bucelas,* Parque Mayer. Eat out on the pavement under a trellis of vines. Again extremely cheap. A meal with wine will cost between 20 and 35 esc.

Restaurante Solmar, Rua das Portas de Santo Antão. Beer and some of the best sea-food in Portugal. Reasonable.

Restaurante António Carlos Barros Bulhosa, Rua Eugénio dos Santos. Rough tables in a wine cellar with speciality of grilled fresh sardines. Excellent value for very little outlay.

There are several theatres in Lisboa. For opera go to the Nacional de S. Carlos, Largo de São Carlos.

Some Useful Addresses in Lisboa:
H.M. Embassy, Rua S. Domingos (Lapa). Tel: 66 11 91.
U.S. Embassy, Avenida Duque de Loulé 39. Tel: 55 51 41.
Main Post Office, Praça dos Restauradores.

Foreign Churches
Church of England. Rua da Estrela 14. Services every Sunday at 8.30 and 11 a.m.
Church of Scotland. Rua Arriaga 13. Services every Sunday at 11 a.m.
Shaaré Tikva Synagogue. Rua Alexandre Herculano 59. Services at 8.30 a.m. and 7 p.m. daily. Saturdays: 9 a.m. and 7 p.m.

Medical
British Hospital. Rua Saraiva de Carvalho 49. Tel: 66 38 37.
Dental Surgery. Clínica Dentária. Estrada Marginal 11, Estoril. Tel: 26 07 75.

Interpreter Guides:

Sindicato Nacional dos Guias-Intérpretes. Rua do Telhal 4. Tel: 36 71 70.
Santarém 78 km, Sintra 28, Porto 328, Ericeira 53.

MAFRA. The main interest of Mafra to the visitor is the enormous monastery and Palace. This fantastic building was built in 1713 by D. João V in fulfilment of a vow if his wife should have a child. It took more than 50,000 men and 1,000 oxen thirteen years to build. It covers 50,000 sq metres and has 4,500 doors and windows. To my mind, the most beautiful part of the building is the library, a great domed room with little windowed alcoves. There are some thirty thousand books in the library, all beautifully bound and tooled. There is a museum of church and monastic furniture and many of the former royal apartments are furnished and open to the public. The church itself is immense and contains marble from every quarry in Portugal. Access to Mafra is by bus or train, but visitors should beware. The station is several miles from the town.
Lisboa 42 km, Sintra 33, Ericeira 11, Cascais 58.

MOLEDO DO MINHO. A village on the left bank of the Rio Minho, fringed by the Galicia mountains. There is a good sandy beach and lovely sea views, including the little rocky island of Insua with its fortress and lighthouse.
Hotels: 1 1st class pensão. Porto 90 km, Viana do Castelo 20, Póvoa de Varzim 61, Braga 67.

MONTE GORDO is a small village that has been transformed by the presence of a large 1st class hotel the *Vasco da Gama.* This 196-room hotel has a swimming pool, motel block, night club and private beach with miles of fine white sand. There are also tennis courts, a children's playground and paddling pool. The village itself has several cheerful little bars.

For people arriving by the train

Algarve fishing boat

is a funicular railway linking the two. On the promontory is the Chapel of Nossa Senhora de Nazaré, originally erected after D. Fuas Roupinho was miraculously saved while following a stag in 1182. You can still see the rock bearing the horse's imprint. The chapel was rebuilt in the 17th century.

Hotels: 1 1st class, the Hotel de Nazaré, *newly opened with a dance floor, snack bar and roof dining room.* 1 3rd class, the Hotel Dom Fuas, *situated on a quiet beach facing the sea. There is a tractor and trailer service connecting the hotel with the town. 8 pensões. Buses to Marinha Grande and Leiria; Alcobaça, Batalha, Coimbra and Porto; Caldas da Rainha, Torres Vedras and Lisboa. Lisboa 129 km, Porto 218.*

from Lisboa, it is best to alight at Vila Real de St. António. Hotel cars will meet the train by arrangement, or you can take a taxi.

Hotels: 1 1st class. Others are being opened. Lisboa 325 km, Spanish frontier at Vila Real de Santo António 4, Tavira 19, Faro 49.

NAZARÉ is probably Portugal's most picturesque resort, with its magnificent crescent-shaped beach dotted with the high-prowed fishing boats very little different from those used by the Phoenicians who founded the village. The local fisher-folk still dress in their traditional costumes and, in spite of the fact that Nazaré is now a popular resort, the whole place retains the atmosphere of a village whose sole *raison d'etre* is fishing. Access, too, is comparatively easy. A train to Valado from Lisboa takes three hours, with a 15-minute bus or taxi connection. Alternatively, there is a bus service from Lisboa which takes about four hours.

The village is divided into two parts, the beach section and the *sitio,* 360 feet above the sea. There

ÓBIDOS. A beautiful old market town still entirely enclosed by the old Moorish ramparts. There is a *Pousada* in the old castle where tourists may stay for up to five nights. See the 14th-century keep, the church of Sta. Maria and just outside the town the church of Senhor da Pedra. If you are in the region on the 3rd May, a *romaria* is held there each year on this date. *Hotels:* Pousada do Castelo, *Estalagen in convent. Lisboa 90 km, Caldas da Rainha 5, Peniche 24.*

OFIR. A small but beautiful seaside resort on the right bank of the Rio Cávado. The nearest shops are at Fão 3 km inland. Ofir is situated in a pine wood and is very popular with British visitors. There is good under-water fishing off the White Horse Rocks.

Hotels: 2 1st class. The Ofir *has dancing, a swimming-pool and a restaurant on the beach. Porto 46 km, Póvoa de Varzim 15, Viana de Castelo 26.*

OLHÃO (pop. 17,000). An industrial centre and fishing port, Olhão is probably best known for the strange cubist construction of its houses, so often seen in paintings and photographs. Although undoubtedly attractive in many ways, the tunny fishing industry and its attendant odours may put off some visitors.

On the outskirts of the town and 300 yards from the sea is the one hotel, the attractive *Estalagem Caique*. They have a restaurant actually on the beach and will arrange fishing trips for guests.
Lisboa 308 km, Faro 10, Tavira 20, São Braz de Alportel 27, Lagos 90.

PENHAS DA SAÚDE. See FUNDÃO.

PENICHE (pop. 9,960). A small fishing port with subsidiary industries of sardine canning and lace making. From here a launch runs daily in the season to the Berlenga Islands. The town is situated on a peninsula about four miles long and three miles wide, linked to the mainland by a stretch of sand about a mile across. At high tide the town is completely surrounded by water. In the centre of the town is the Citadel, with town walls, massive doors, ramparts and towers. The ramparts date back to 1557, but the remainder of the defences are 17th-century. On the mainland nearby there are very fine grottos and rock formations.
Hotels: 2 1st class pensões. Lisboa 95 km, Caldas da Rainha 29, Leiria 86, Figueira da Foz 138, Santarém 85.

PORTALEGRE (pop. 10,500). Situated on one of the main Madrid to Lisboa roads, Portalegre stands high in the foothills of the Serra which divides Spain from Portugal. The Cathedral has an imposing 18th-century façade, and there is a small but interesting museum in the Town Hall which has some good polychrome terra cotta bas reliefs and some furniture and pictures.
Lisboa 233 km, Spanish frontier 24, Estremoz 55, Alpalhão 22, Abrantes 80.

PORTIMÃO is an attractive little country town with a bustling fishing port. Of the 4 estalagens, the *Miradouro* is especially good.
Hotels: 4 estalagens, 1 pensão. Lisboa 288 km, Praia da Rocha 3.

PORTINHO DA ARRÁBIDA. Close to Sesimbra, this is a delightful spot with a secluded bay of white sand, backed by the sweeping hills of the Serra da Arrábida. The village itself is extremely small and there is only one estalagem. Consequently this is a place for beach lovers, walkers and fishermen. There are some interesting excursions in the vicinity, such as the tiny chapel in the Grotto Santa Margarida, Palmela Castle and the ancient Phoenician ruins at Troia.

Boats at Nazaré

Portinho da Arrábida

Botanists and geologists may care to join the speculation as to whether some of the unusual flora, fauna and rock formations found near Portinho da Arrábida support the theory of the lost land of Atlantis.

Hotels: Estalagem Santa Maria, *part of which is an old converted fort on the water's edge. Buses to Sesimbra. No direct service to Lisboa. Lisboa 38 km.*

PORTO (OPORTO) (pop. 305,450). This is the second largest city in Portugal and an important commercial port and industrial city. During the times of the Goths it was made a bishopric, but during the 8th century it suffered heavily at the hands of the Moors.

The city was freed in the 12th century and became capital of the Northern Kingdom. In the 15th century its shipyards built many of the vessels for Henry the Navigator's voyages of discovery. Porto has a history of revolutions. In 1628 and again in 1661 the population revolted against heavy taxes and in 1756 against the wine monopoly given by Pombal to the Upper Douro Wine Company. During the 18th century the town grew rich on its wine trade, but the French armies occupied Porto from 1808 to 1809. The great liberal revolution of 1820 began in Porto, and in 1820 the town revolted against the reactionary government of Dom Miguel. There followed a long and costly blockade of the city which lasted until 1833. Prosperity soon returned, however, and Porto has been a busy industrial centre ever since.

The city is built on the hills rising some 5 km from the mouth of the Rio Douro. A bridge connects Porto with Vila Nova de Gaia on the other side of the river with its ancient wine lodges.

Porto is not itself a seaside resort, but it has excellent hotels, good communications and is a useful centre for visiting the resorts to the north, as well as such places as Braga, Barcelos, Guimarães and the upper valley of the Douro. There is a tram service to Foz do Douro, which has a pleasant sandy beach.

The Cedofeita Church. By tradition its foundation dates back to King Theodomir and the year A.D. 556 but experts consider that it was in all probability built in the 12th century. There is some rich carving on the capitals of the north and west doors.

Porto: Cedofeita Church

Church of the Tertian Carmelite Order. Decorated in black, white and gold, this church used to be famous for its Good Friday procession. The figures used in it are still preserved in the church.

The Sé (Cathedral) has square towers at each corner, making it look more like a fortress than a church. Originally built in the 12th and 13th centuries, it was heavily restored in the 17th and 18th centuries and little of the Romanesque exterior remains intact. The rose window is probably 13th-century and the statue of Nossa Senhora de Vendôme in the Chapel of Sao Vicente shows the influence of the French decorators of the period. The Gothic cloister is graceful and has a facing of fine *azulejos,* but I found both the Capela Môr and the Chapel of the Holy Sacrament to be heavy and over-decorated. They are, however, much admired by some connoisseurs.

Torre dos Clerigos (next to the Cathedral). The Tower is the highest in Portugal and was built by Niccolo Nazzoni in 1748. It is of granite and attached to a church, which though of pleasant lines is otherwise undistinguished. There is a wonderful view from the belfry.

The Bishop's Palace. This vast building, rebuilt in 1772, is now the town hall. There is a hall of mirrors, a fine staircase and some paintings on the first floor.

The Misericórdia Church. Built by Nazzoni in the 18th century, it is of grey granite and has a beautiful white plaster ceiling. In the Brotherhood of Santa Casa da Misericórdia next door is one of the most important works of art in Portugal, the celebrated painting—*Fons Vitae.*

This is attributed to Bernard van Orly and is dated about 1520. It shows Christ on the Cross between the Blessed Virgin and St John, with the blood of the Saviour flowing onto D. Manoel I and his wife and children.

Convent of St Clare. Quite close to the Cathedral. The exterior is quite plain, but the interior is lined with gold. There are some very fine coloured statues and a high-relief of the Last Judgement.

Church of Sao Francisco. The original building was erected in the 13th century, rebuilt in the 14th century and again in the 17th and 18th centuries. During the 17th and 18th centuries it was highly decorated with gilded wood and there is scarcely a foot not covered with angels and cherubs, fruit and flowers, birds and animals. In the Chapel of St John the Baptist there is a 16th-century painting of Christ's baptism, while in another chapel there is a good 15th-century Italian fresco.

Two worthwhile buildings outside the city limits can be reached quite easily by tram and foot. Palácio do Freixo is a fine 18th-century château, probably built by Nazzoni. There is a wonderful view of the Douro valley from the grounds. Take the number 11 or 12 tram to Campanha Station. It is then about 15 minutes' walk.

The Convent of Nossa Senhora do Pilar is a domed church dating back to 1598. It is now a barracks. To reach the convent, take a 13 or 14 tram to the Dom Luís Bridge. The convent stands to the left after the bridge.

Rua do Infante Henrique is a street containing much of interest, including the 'factory' house of the Port Wine Industry, erected in 1785

The Church of the Carmelites, Porto

by William Whitehead, the British Consul of the time. The heads of the various wine shipping companies still meet there for a weekly lunch. At the end of the street, in the square, is a monument to Prince Henry and just around the corner in the Rua da Alfândega is the old Customs House, which is supposed to stand on the spot where he was born. Also in the square is the Bolsa or Stock Exchange.

Museums. Museu Nacional de Soares dos Reis. The house itself is of considerable interest. During the Peninsular War it served first as the French headquarters and then as Wellington's. The exhibits are well-arranged and there is a particularly good collection of pottery, porcelain and ceramics. Of the pictures, the most interesting are the pastels by Pillement and some Clouet panels. There is also a collection of coins, including a 5th-century head of Arethusa in gold. Casa-Museu Guerra Junqueiro in Rua D. Hugo was once the home of the well-known Portuguese poet and writer. There is a collection of furniture, carpets, silver and pottery of the 14th to 18th centuries.

Useful Addresses.
Portuguese State Tourist Dept., C.D.T., Praça Dom João 1, 25-4°.
Main Post Office, Praça da Batalha.
British Consulate, Praça Dom Joao 1.
American Consulate, Rua Sá Bandeira 605.
British Hospital, Rua da Bandeir-inha 12.
Church of England Church, Largo da Maternidade.
British Institute. Rua do Bryner 79.
Hotels: 2 de luxe class, Hotel Infante Sagres, *small but luxurious, created out of a lovely private mansion; quite outstanding in service and comfort, with beautiful period furniture. 3 1st class, 1 2nd class, 4 3rd class, many pensoes. Lisboa 328 km, Braga 50, Aveiro 70, Viseu 138, Viana do Castelo 72, Vila Real 115.*

PORTO BRANDÃO. A fishing village just across the Rio Tejo from Lisboa. Reached by ferry. The Lazaretto, once the quarantine station for Lisboa, is a huge building now used as a home for children. There are pleasant walks in the vicinity but nothing to attract one to stay there.

PÓVOA DE VARZIM. A fishing port and popular seaside resort, Póvoa de Varzim has a large sandy beach, a casino licensed for gambling, a bullring and a race track. There is a very attractive old fishermen's quarter.
Hotels: 1 1st class, 1 pensão.
Trains: Minho line. Buses to Vila do Conde, Porto, Esposende, Viana do Castelo, Braga, Guimaraes and Barcelos. Porto 30 km, Viana do Castelo 41, Vila do Conde 4.

Póvoa de Varzim

PRAIA DA CAPARICA. Reached by crossing the Rio Tejo by ferry boat from Lisboa, this little resort-cum-fishing village is only fifteen minutes away by bus. There is a wide beach stretching for some 25 km which is backed by pine woods. There are plenty of gay little cafés in the village and some good shops. It is an excellent place to spend a quiet, relaxing holiday, with the advantage of being close to Lisboa. Not a place for those seeking night-life as there is none locally and the last bus is at midnight. The new bridge across the river is due to be completed in 1967 and this whole area will then become more popular and developed.
Hotels: 1 1st class, 1 estalagem, 3 pensões. Lisboa 12 km, Porto 341.

PRAIA DA ROCHA. Famous for its fantastic beach backed by weirdly shaped cliffs, Praia da Rocha has been known as a watering place since Edwardian times. At first sight the beach looks small, but eventually the visitor discovers that there is a whole series of bays each separated from the next by arches and columns of rock. The sand is golden and slopes gently, allowing safe bathing for the smallest children. Access to Praia da Rocha by road or rail is via Portimão. There are taxis available at the station, and hotel cars will meet trains by arrangement. There is a restaurant overlooking the sea, a casino and tennis courts.

The *Pensão Sol* is modern and spotlessly clean but is very often full up. The *Pinguim* is owned by an English family with children and is therefore more suitable for families.
Hotels: 1 1st class, 1 2nd class, 3 estalagens, 3 pensões. Portimão 3 km, Lisboa 288.

PRAIA DAS MAÇÃS. This little resort is set among beautiful scenery, near Cabo da Roca, the most westerly point of Continental Europe, and within sight of the heights of Sintra. There are several good beaches, the main one having a lido with a swimming pool, dance hall and tea terrace. Tennis courts are in the course of preparation. The resort is a wonderful centre, with Lisboa, Estoril, Sintra, Ericeira and Batalha all within easy reach. Slightly inland and on the way to Cabo da Roca is the elegant little village of **Colares** with villas, 2 *pensões* and 2 *estalagens* set amongst pine trees. The village is noted for its wine.
Hotels: 1 estalagem, 1 pensao. Lisboa 39 km.

PRAIA DE MIRAMAR. A popular spot for the townspeople from Porto. A pleasant beach backed by villas. There is a golf course, and nearby at Gandara Park, tennis courts and a casino.
Porto 16 km, Braga 66, Aveiro 54, Vila Real 131.

QUARTEIRA. A pleasant little fishing village, popular with Portu-

Praia da Rocha

guese holidaymakers. There are several little bars and restaurants, a lovely beach and a picturesque fish market. Being so near to the airport at Faro, there are plans for several new hotels, but at the moment the only beds are to be found in two small but well run pensões.

Lisboa 312 km, Faro 20, Loulé 6.

QUELUZ. A pleasant drive from the capital, a train from Rossio station or a bus will take you to this enchanting palace. Started in 1758 by D. Pedro, the palace was designed by Matheus Vicente de Oliveira and the landscaping was done by a Frenchman, Jean Baptiste Robillon. The whole palace is open to the public, though the Government still uses it for entertaining important visitors. The Queen and The Duke of Edinburgh stayed here on their official visit and must have enjoyed strolling in the lovely formal gardens with wonderful examples of topiary, delicate balustrades and groups of statues.

Lisboa 15 km.

SAGRES. From here you can look across the bay to Cape St Vincent, where Rodney defeated the Spanish fleet in 1770 and together Nelson

Henry the Navigator

and Jarvis beat the French in 1797. Sagres with its sheltered harbour is on the eastern side of the Cape. It was here that Prince Henry the Navigator established his school of navigation which resulted in his sailors discovering so many new lands. Among his pupils were Christopher Columbus and Vasco da Gama.

The angling at Sagres is particularly good and it is a good centre for snorkel fishing, dove and pigeon shooting.

Access to Sagres is from Lagos station. From there there is a frequent bus service or hotels will arrange transfers at a cost of about 120 esc (£1 10s. or $4.75).

The *Hotel Baleeira* (1st class), is especially suitable for fishermen. It has a fishermen's room with scales, refrigerator and storage facilities for heavy gear. The hotel has boats for hire and fishing excursions can be arranged. There is also the fine new *Pousada do Infante*. This is extremely comfort-

Sagres

able, has excellent food and is very reasonably priced. Finally there is an excellent small pensão, the *Infante Sagres*, costing about 140 esc (£1 15s. or $5.00) per day for two people including meals.
Lisboa 288 km, Lagos 32, Faro 113.

SÃO MARTINHO DO PORTO. A delightful small resort situated on an almost landlocked bay. The swimming is absolutely safe, and there is good sailing, boating, fishing and duck shooting. Just inland from Sao Martinho on the main Porto-Lisboa road is **Alfeizerão** which has a first-rate *pousada* perched on the side of a hill with a good view of the sea.
Hotels: 1 2nd class, the Hotel Parque. *This is very comfortable with two tennis courts, miniature golf course and dancing, open 1st June to end of September. 3 pensãoes. Trains: Western Line. Buses to Nazaré, Caldas da Rainha, Torres Vedras, Lisboa. Lisboa 101 km.*

SANTARÉM (pop. 14,000). Conquered by the Moors in the 7th century, Santarém was not recaptured until the advent of the Crusaders in the 12th century. The city is built on a hill above the Rio Tejo and just outside the town is the longest bridge in Portugal.

Architecturally, there are many pleasing buildings in Santarém, but nothing of really outstanding importance. A rather sad little story about the former Church of S. João de Alporão makes a visit interesting. It was built by a nobleman's wife as a tomb for her husband. Unfortunately his body was hacked into pieces by the Moors and all that remained for her to bury was one tooth now contained in his tomb.

The former Jesuit College, the Church of N. S. de Piedade and the Church of Marvila are other buildings of interest.
Hotels: 1 2nd class, 1 3rd class. Lisboa 78 km, Caldas da Rainha 58, Tomar 67.

Santarém: Gothic fountain

SANTIAGO DO CACÉM. An inland village on the main Lisboa-Lagos road. I mention it because of the excellent *Pousada de São Tiago* which makes a useful stop on the drive from Lisboa to the Algarve.
Lisboa 141 km, Setúbal 101, Sines 17, Lagos 125.

SÃO BRAZ DE ALPORTEL (pop. 11,000) is a small market town set in the midst of the delightful Algarve countryside. The *Pousada de Sao Braz* is just outside the town (5 km) and makes a good base from which to explore the charming white villages of the area. It specialises in regional dishes—mainly fish.
Faro 17 km, Tavira 22, Lagos 82, Ferreira do Alentejo 124.

SÃO PEDRO DE MUEL. This tiny village has become a centre for artists. There is a wild craggy coast line with a choice of several small but good beaches. The resort is being developed and plans are in hand for a new hotel, casino etc. Access from Lisboa by train is easy, the nearest station being Marinha Grande a few miles away. Onward connection is by bus or taxi. Nearby, is the Pinhal de Leiria, Portugal's largest forest which provides the raw material for a thriving turpentine industry.

Hotels: 3 1st class pensões, the prices from 110 esc (£1 7s. 6d. or $4.40) per day for a double room. Lisboa 150 km.

Cliffs at Sesimbra

SEIXAL. Situated in a bay on the opposite side of the river from Lisboa, this small town is most attractive seen from the ferry. It consists, in the main, of many tidal mills, now mostly in a state of decay. Picturesque for painters but definitely not a resort.

São Braz

SESIMBRA (pop. 6,880). On the south side of the Rio Tejo, Sesimbra has retained its atmosphere of being an unspoilt fishing village—yet is in fact a popular resort. There is a very good sandy beach backed by imposing cliffs, and there are plenty of little bays and coves which you can have to yourself. It is possible to hire boats for fishing expeditions and enthusiasts will find excellent sport with bass, bream, red and grey mullet, swordfish and tunny. There are also several pleasant bays close by which can be reached by boat for picnics and swimming parties. By way of entertainment, there is *fado* in the evenings at one of the small restaurants and you can dance at one of the hotels. The fish market is definitely worth a visit with its public auction of the catch.

The Castelo de Sesimbra now consists of some restored walls enclosing the remains of the old Moorish city. The Church of Nossa Senhora do Castelo is 12th-century. In Sesimbra itself, the woodwork, sculpture and paintings in the Misericórdia church are 16th and 17th-century.

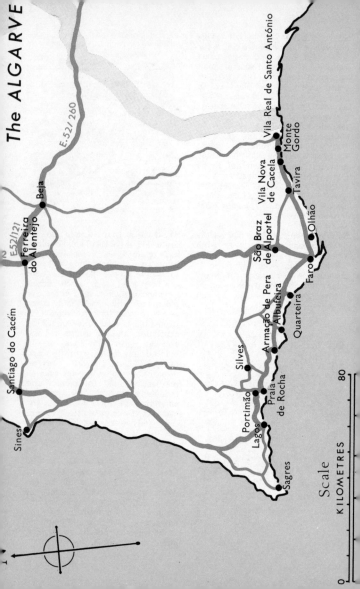

The ALGARVE

E.52/ 260

Beja

E52/121

2

Ferreira do Alentejo

Santiago do Cacém

Sines

Vila Real de Santo António

Monte Gordo

Tavira

Vila Nova de Cacela

São Braz de Alportel

Olhão

Faro

Armação de Pera

Albufeira

Quarteira

Silves

Portimão

Praia de Rocha

Lagos

Sagres

Scale

KILOMETRES

0   80

Hotels: 1 1st class, 1 2nd class, 1 1st class pensao. Buses to Cacilhas (hourly service). This connects with the ferry for Lisboa. Last ferry from Lisboa connecting with a bus leaves at 9.30 p.m. but taxis at the pier-head will take you to Sesimbra for about 80 esc (£1 or $2.80). Lisboa 20 km.

SETÚBAL (pop. 44,000). An
industrial town and an important
fishing port, Setúbal makes an
excellent centre for touring, rather
than being a resort in its own
right. Facilities include a theatre,
a bullring and tennis courts.
Opposite Setúbal on the other bank
of the Rio Sado, are the beaches of
Troia.

   With the building of the proposed
bridge across the Rio Tejo from
Lisboa, it is likely that this whole
area will be re-developed.
Buses to Portinho da Arrábida (during summer months). Lisboa 33 km, Evora 104, Santiago do Cacém 101.

SILVES (pop. 11,000) makes an
interesting drive from any of the
resorts on the Algarve coast.
Originally a Moorish town, it was

Silves

destroyed in the 16th century by an
earthquake. However, there remain
the great water cisterns, food
storage cellars and much of the
Moorish Castle. There is no
accommodation of tourist standard.
Portimao 25 km.

SINES (pop. 5,000). Roughly half-
way between Lisboa and Cape
St Vincent, this picturesque fishing
village makes a convenient stopping
place on the drive down to the

Sines

Algarve. The little harbour is
tucked away under the cliffs, while
the village itself straggles up the
hill-side. There are plenty of little
coves and bays near-by, all of
which have excellent sheltered
bathing. Fishing is extremely good,
especially for tunny and swordfish.

   The Chapel of Nossa Senhora das
Sales was rebuilt by Vasco da
Gama and finished in 1529 after his
death. The chapel is only open
these days on August 15th for the
feast of the Assumption. Sines is the
birthplace of Vasco da Gama and
there is a commemorative tablet
on the site of the house where he was
born.
Hotels: 4 pensões. Trains: there is a through carriage on some trains from Lisboa, about 4 hours journey.

Buses to surrounding towns and to Setúbal. Lisboa 159 km, Santiago do Cacém 17, Beja 95.

SINTRA. Really three separate villages, Sintra is the most interesting excursion that can be done comfortably in a day from Lisboa. It is reached by bus from Estoril and Cascais. From Lisboa you take a train from Rossio Station. From Sintra station it is a ten minute walk to the village or you can take one of the trams or buses marked 'Vila'.

All three villages tower above the surrounding countryside and have fantastic views. Each way you look, follies and castles crown every peak and crag. Lush vegetation and sub-tropical flowers flourish in strange contrast to the stony fields in the plain below.

In the lower village, Sintra itself, are the main hotels, the Royal Palace, now a museum, and the Misericórdia Hospital. The *Seteais Hotel* is about a mile away from the square on the Monserrate road. The palace is Moorish in

Sintra

origin, but has been added to extensively since. There are some very fine *azulejos*, some interesting portraits and some good porcelain. The garden with its formal terraces is very attractive and would be a good spot for a picnic.

Up the hill you come to the two villages of Santa Maria and São Pedro. Santa Maria is a little cluster of cottages, apparently glued to the side of the mountain. Take the leafy lane past the convent and you reach São Pedro de Sintra. Here in the large square by the church there is held a market-cum-fair on the 2nd and 4th Sundays of each month. If you can arrange your visit to coincide with one of the fairs, do so, for they are amusing and gay and you may even be able to buy a bargain at one of the antique stalls.

On the very highest peak of all, reached by a winding path is the Pena Palace. The palace was rebuilt in the middle of the 19th century on the site of an old monastery. A beautiful little cloister still remains. The remainder can be only described as mock Scottish Baronial in the worst possible taste. Red plush vies with ugly heavy furniture and there is even one room where the cement walls have been laboriously hand-painted to resemble wood. Even so the palace is interesting, giving an insight into the way the Royal Family must have lived.

The *Palacio dos Seteais,* a delightful hotel, is really an 18th-century palace, beautifully furnished with period pieces and carefully restored. The drawing room was painted by Pillement and the great majority of the frescoes are originals. Considering the great comfort and excellent food the hotel is not expensive at between 280 esc (£3 10s. or $9.60) and 420 esc (£5 5s. or $14.50) per day full pension.

*Other hotels: 2 3rd class (the
Central in the square has good food),
6 pensões. Lisboa 30 km, Ericeira
22, Cascais 25.*

TAVIRA (pop. 12,500). A Moorish
looking town at the mouth of the
Rio Séqua, it was partially destroyed
by an earthquake in 1755. Even so
there are some fine tiles, a beautiful
Renaissance doorway and fine
wooden altars in the Misericórdia
church. At nearby Santa Luzia was
found a 1st-century Greek inscrip-
tion.
*Hotels: 2 small 2nd class pensões.
Monte Gordo 19 km, Faro 30.*

TOMAR (11,500). This is nowadays
a busy industrial town with paper
mills and cotton factories. From a
tourist point of view it is famous
because it contains the Convent of
Christ, the great Templar's Monastery. The round church dates back
to the 12th century and the seven
cloisters range in period from the
12th to the 17th centuries. The
cemetery cloister was built by

Tomar

Henry the Navigator, but one of
the most attractive is the two-
storey cloister of the Filipes. Up-
stairs is the dormitory with the
cells leading off it. The main part
of the convent is now used as a
college for young missionaries.
*Hotels: 1 3rd class, 2 estalagens, 1
pensão. Lisboa 148 km, Leiria 45,
Coimbra 115, Santarém 67.*

VALENÇA DO MINHO (pop.
3,000) lies above the Rio Minho
which forms Portugal's northern
border with Spain. Thirty-one
kilometres south of Vigo, it is on
the main coast road to Porto
(126 km) and is overlooked by a fine
old frontier fort. The *Pousada de
São Teotonio* has some dozen
rooms with their own bathroom.
*Hotels: 1 pensão, 1 pousada. Porto
126 km, Viana do Castelo 52.*

VIANA DO CASTELO (pop.
14,130). A beautiful and historic
town situated on the right bank
of the Rio Lima near the sea.
Behind the town rises Monte de
Santa Luzia, which in spring is
covered in mimosa. There is a rack
and pinion railway line to the sum-
mit. The beach is sandy.
The church of São Bento,
decorated with rich carvings and
azulejos, was built in 1545 and rebuilt in 1710. The parish church,
built between 1400 and 1440, is
Romanesque in style. To the left
of the church is an old house with a
coat of arms, called João Velho.
Opposite is another old house with
armorial bearings dating back to
the 16th century.
The Town Hall in the Praça da
República dates back to 1502. On
the north side of the square is the
Misericórdia built in 1589, and the
Igreja da Misericórdia rebuilt in
1714. In the centre of the square is a
beautiful fountain designed by
João Lopes O Velho. To the side

Viana do Castelo

glorious sandy beach, and is near Povoa de Varzim with its casino, bullring and race track. The town is a centre for regional dancing and folk-lore. There is a thriving sardine canning industry and lots of local colour. On a hill overlooking the river is the huge convent of Santa Clara, founded in 1318. There are numerous tombs in the Manuel-ine funeral chapel. The parish church of São João was built between 1500 and 1518, but the clock tower is of a much later period, probably 17th - century. Along the river road at Rio Mau is the old church of Sao Cristóvão dating back to 1151.

Hotels: 1 1st class, The Palacio, extremely comfortable with beach restaurant and tennis. Boats on the Rio Ave can be arranged. Trains: Minho line. Buses to Porto, Póvoa de Varzim, Esposende and Viana do Castelo. Porto 27 km, Póvoa de Varzim 4, Viana do Castelo 45.

of the Misericórdia is the Palace of the Counts of Carreira and past it the former convent of Santa Ana, which was built in 1515 and rebuilt in the period 1898 to 1907. The Church of São Domingos has a beautiful 16th-century façade. Near-by the museum-library houses a collection of paintings, historical remains and archaeological speci-mens in rooms panelled with fine old *azulejos*.

Hotels: Hotel Santa Luzia (1st class). Sponsored by the C D.T. Private swimming-pool and glorious views. Car service to the town and beach. 1 3rd class, 2 pensões. Market day: Friday. Festivals: Nossa Senhora da Agonia, 15th-17th August; Santa Luzia, 3rd Sunday in June. Trains: Minho Line. Buses to Braga, Esposende, Póvoa de Varzim, Vila do Conde, Porto. Porto 72 km, Lisboa 400, Póvoa de Varzim 41, Braga 47.

VILA DO CONDE. This is a colourful little fishing port with a

Vila do Conde

VILA FRANCA DE XIRA (pop. 9,000). This ancient town on the banks of the Tagus is an important road centre as the Carmona bridge (named after the former Portuguese president) is the nearest one to Lisboa and thus a vital north-south link. The town is chiefly known for its bullring and fighting bulls are bred in the countryside to the east. Vila Franca is a good place for a night out from Lisboa as there are two *estalagens*—the *Estalagem do Gado Bravo* is first class—the restaurants serve local specialities, and in the bars you can usually hear the mournful *fado*. *Hotels:* 2 estalagens. Lisboa 31 km.

VILA NOVA DE CACELA. A tiny village less than a kilometre from the magnificent beach at Manta Rota. The village is mentioned here because of the little inn called *A Ameixoeira* (the Plum Tree), an enchanting establishment run by a young Englishman and an enthusiastic Portuguese staff. The food is excellent, the atmosphere young and gay. Prices are extremely reasonable. *Monte Gordo 8 km.*

VILA PRAIA DE ÂNCORA. A small seaside resort near the mouth of the Rio Minho. There is an exceptionally large rise and fall of tide and bathing is only good at high tide. *Hotels:* 1 1st class pensao. Porto 85 km, Viana do Castelo 15.

VILA REAL (pop. 9,323). Founded in 1288 by D. Diniz, the town is the centre of a rich farming district with many vineyards. It is very attractive with lovely old houses, many of which date back to the 16th century and have armorial bearings. The Cathedral of São Domingos is Gothic and has a fine gold reredos. The interior of the Church of São Pedro has some rich ceilings and gold woodwork es-

pecially in front of the chancel arch. Below Vila Real near the deserted and ruined Carmo church is the delightful little 16th-century Chapel of St Anthony.

I find Vila Real a most attractive little town with an atmosphere all of its own. If you have a chance to visit it, you may find it useful to use the *Pousada de S. Gonçalo* at Amarante. *Porto 115 km, Amarante 49, Lamego 40, Guimarães 82.*

VILA REAL DE S. ANTÓNIO. This small town founded by the Marquês de Pombal is a frontier town between Spain and Portugal. On the Spanish side of the Rio Guardiana lies Ayamonte. The two towns are linked by a car ferry and steamer service which runs quite frequently up until dusk.

Vila Real is a centre of the tunny fishing industry and tourists with strong stomachs can watch the fish being driven into a cage of nets before being speared in a bloody carnage. *Hotels:* 1 2nd class, 1 pensão. *Lisboa 329 km, Sevilla (Spain) 154, Tavira 23; Faro 53.*

VISEU (pop. 13,000). A pretty little town with winding streets, old manorial houses and little baroque palaces. The Cathedral has a 16th-century exterior, but much of the inside is the original 12th-century building. The chancel and sacristy both have richly painted ceilings and the Gothic doorway to the chapter house is particularly lovely. The city is justly proud of its Grão Vasco Museum which contains a magnificent collection of Primitive paintings and some fine sculptures. *Hotels:* 1 1st, 1 2nd class; 1 1st class estalagem, 3 pensões. Porto 138 km, Lamego 70, Vila Real 110.

Viseu

INDEX

*All places which have a main entry, and the pages on
which these occur, are printed in heavy type.
The page numbers in colour are map references.
Asterisks indicate illustrations.*